Beverly Dahlen

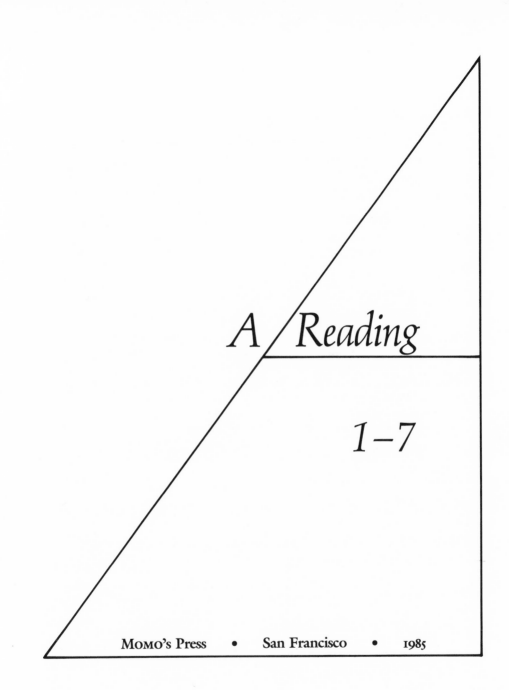

A Reading

1–7

MOMO's Press • San Francisco • 1985

Library of Congress Cataloging in Publication Data

Dahlen, Beverly.
  A Reading (1–7).

  I. Title. II. Title: A Reading (one to seven)
PS3554.A27R4 1985   811'.54   85-15235
ISBN 0-917672-23-2

Excerpts from this work have been previously published (in some cases in slightly different form) in *Feminist Studies* (Summer, 1980), *# Magazine* (December, 1981), *Feminist Poetics: A Consideration of the Female Construction of Language* (edited by Kathleen Fraser, 1984), and in the *Medicine Bundle/ Magabark* project, in which pages of text are incorporated into "A Portrait of Edgar Allan Poe," a sculpture by William Geis. For the provision of a residency during the month of August, 1983, the author thanks the Briarcombe Foundation, Bolinas California.

The author gratefully acknowledges the attentiveness of her editors and collaborators.

Book design and cover by Mary Ann Hayden. Photograph of author by Marcia Miner.

Phototypeset in Galliard and Palatino types by Michele Thomas at Type By Design, Fairfax, California.

Funding for this publication was made possible partially by a grant from the National Endowment for the Arts, a Federal Agency. MOMO's Press is a project of Intersection, San Francisco.

MOMO's Press • 45 Sheridan Street • San Francisco CA 94103

A Reading 1–7

"Wittgenstein asked where, when, and by what rationally established criterion the process of free yet potentially linked and significant association in psychoanalysis could be said to have a stop. An exercise in 'total reading' is also potentially unending."

— GEORGE STEINER
After Babel

One

before that and before that. everything in a line. where it was broken into, the house. not a body but still I could not see that it didn't have a roof. then there was something to cry about. assumption of protection. whether I thought the sky the top of. whatever does. this I carry forward. the sky which was not a limit but apparently so. and that mistake which. colored it. what color? as if in another light. so shadows.

it was required that a number of complicated actions were to be performed in a certain sequence. it would get you there. she who goes back in a straight line. the illusion of irrelevance. so that we could trace it ticking. single minded. the sun now coming clear of the clouds nearest us and sharper lines. this goes black and white. I won't count it.

thrawn. had from out there as if a giant hand. the persistence of that. why in the dark, 'crippled, misshapen,' flung into the game, broken, a counter. gnostic. *deus absconditus.*

how forever and away I would wonder if this came from anywhere, or if floating unconnected. as clouds seem to. mysterious powers now visible. rest in that, as water now solid, air more so, she flies. impinging on another time.

cut-ups. hath made fools of us all. and excellent fooling, to be so fooled.

knife track. cutting it. this fat hand. turning in time same as. his which I see, more than his name. the stubborn inheritance. that which persists. a will which changes.

there in the squawk and whistle of the bird, motors pulling. this to step to the next one. how out there an old breathlessness about the sea rising. or falling. falling into the stream. not to make the leap. what, to miss a step. some rhythm unheard.

cat herding. eyes down. that cut off. beyond which. how she was a nerve to me. how quickly. she, some other, takes place. goes and is lost.

cornucopia: a readiness to provide all that is needed, that abundance, that fertility. choking. lighting up one side of the face only. casting what else into shadow.

the deprivations. the glut.

continued. this was an echo. the double. claustrophobia. an illness in which one suffocates, closing in, there seem to be. overwhelmingly. always the word ready at the tip. our lack of conviction. the exaggeration. the more we don't the more we.

now looking back but not wanting to trace the way: the forest closed behind her. the trees, sinister, consciously malevolent, clasping branches behind one's back. that reading. or casting out. the powers that oppose us. now clearly visible. the source is not split, it is not older than we are.

finding it, how know it. everything else unchosen. waste. to settle our differences. to count up all the bills in separate piles. exchange value. what use. everything else thrown away. under a spell. the end of trailing clouds of glory. or its other: the hand in darkness, flinging. as if mud. excrement. to have done with the judgment of childhood. that haunting. that echo. hearing him in it: Artaud. an illness perhaps so old there would be no

—

a dream of whose murder. afterward she lay there, a bank of gray clouds growing.

having chosen whether there is no ocean.

the way of the boundary the way of the flood. her face in the dark window dark how she saw it and spelled me.

a fragment of an analysis: it was so easy to knock her out just like the movies she asked for it. bonk on the head she was done for. but someone righteous and Spanish saw it from an upper window. we were caught. how bare-faced.

all those women. how they tried to be a conscience for one another. how lying seemed their native tongue.

not to say William, bilious, not to echo, repeat what won't come clear, not to be caught here in sticking in the throat. gagging. the saying not to say. we covered it up but were found out anyway. it was done in the open. that's where the wind comes, for wind read calm, and the darkness, and for darkness read light. that's where she is one or another so must be both. the murdered or murderer.

think of it. choosing chooses all. drags in the cat's tail Arcturus far star clouds of glory. this is talk. talk is cheap.

the interminable reading. the infinite analysis.

—

a strange clock ticking. as if time were flung out, a canopy unrolled. the sky. the illusory thing. the idea is not in it. the idea is. elsewhere. among us. floating around, she said.

jesuitical. a veritable excuse. this blind. once gone forever forgotten. retrieved. or a fish. awash. the light begins to play. brobbling. or foaming in the chest. each broken bubble.

each shell splitting in the air. moreover. and came down to a valley. just at twilight. it lengthened. filigree. or an afterthought. an afterimage. did she see that? head turning. we held no brief for. going down. a spinoff. a cylinder. somehow music.

unjustified it by saying it was the piece itself and not so much that we were encountering for the first time anything new but rather that you would have gone to sleep otherwise. *ho* hum. and you could not hold in your head the beginning of that sentence together with the end. we were talking about following it. we were talking. I am preparing in the most banal way to say everything possible.

one needn't follow it. we were walking but then the sun went down. had no we were walking over ridges and lavas. the brains of the backyard. wholly unaccountable. I was looking for a line I said. in the old days. the place was so new, it was so new, it was old. like the beginning of the world. it was that new.

—

writing I was sitting there the cat and the light saw it for the first time that day the light in gray or the sandy shadows. a tin pot. there was chimney. there was the chimney. the looking on of it, the opening to another world. it was a chimney in a gray roof. the side of her thigh. here forever, gone for awhile.

dreams, we think what has gone out of this world. thinking about it. the man with the socks. the light. an airplane. all the old. what was tried and failed. a life unveiled. taking off the clothes. never meant to. what. I never meant to hurt her. we were holding candles in the dark. we were opening doors in a dark house. the first day we were here. it was raining. of course it was raining. it would always be raining there. we would take care of business. the outer world is different from the other one. contrary. it needed to be sustained. this was as dark as digesting food in. that goes on. we never think of it. it goes on. it goes on by itself. nothing need interfere with it. think of her as a corpse. the failure. failed. something failed in the dark.

heart. take heart. it was a stone. stone dropped into a pool. silent. not thrown. the stone somehow got in from outside. falling there. it failed. we would all fail in some way like that. no man knoweth the day or the hour.

the end of a trope. the end of a turning. the end of a facing to the light. lost to a darkness utterly. underscored. what was in the bass line. the beat it played unheard. the sound of that ragtime.

whatever you would take, mother named me *Elsie* when she called. little daughter, she was me to her, we were all sisters. we would all be sisters in the same family.

in those rooms. wandering with crowds of strangers.

nothing. what were you thinking? nothing. all those things. the cherry tree, it being summertime. turning first to the chapter on mourning and melancholia and later to the chapter on the uncanny. this was about mirrors. in some sense she was my double. she died.

moving in some shadow the light seems just beyond the edge of. moving sparely the flesh falling away. willing I had given my hand, there was my hand on it. the figure of her among the trees which I always remember as a photograph. why we walk into death after photography. ah, so, they will say, will have said, she is sleeping. they have masked the marks of choking, how she must have gagged and strangled at the end, and laid her face to rest. they will have done that. so at the end there will be a picture, that image, that lie.

—

mew the doorjamb I was going to say but stopped and thought about it was it fair. in the dream there was a storekeeper there was something round, there was something round.

the thing which was there is not a word but words track it. 'memory-trace.'

its deterioration. breaking down. the reconstruction. words trace it. *tracer of lost persons.*

what in the round, that gave roundness to it, the daily round, it was when I saw the round bowl, the cup, the orange, round, and began it.

began it again, and his name in the book, that took me back. somehow I had been thinking how he was caught in the mirror, the infinite doubling so that even at the end. coming and going the glass face. the three wounds and their denial.

everything piled on top of everything else in the staircase, I don't like it. already the glass box is a memory-trace. the thing below the surface. the region of my mother's country. it was familiar. it was strange. hermetically sealed. the dream of the place, *déjà vu*, at night, a park, lighted lanterns hung among the trees. we were strolling.

weather wandering or clearing the sun. there from shadows, inside and outside. everything spun out but now you could photograph that. the child in the veil, inside and outside. he said: taking pictures inside the womb is nothing sacred?

to fix the graystair the round window the porthole. the red the wrap. to hold fast to the tree. to center the serve, to bring the dinner. having a thought the same as having a baby. it comes from inside, unreal. the fountain. that's what we remember. we were supposed to be golden. each one a savior. that would redeem it. no one told us so.

marriage the winter, hold whether the thing is true. hold in proportion not to the truth. hold on, holding on to it. came out of the door, looked up, it was darkening. it was darkening I thought last night painting my eyelids. that was the origin of that thought. I thought it. I wrote it down. that became the thought I thought. forever after that. that written down thought became my thought. whenever.

we do not love words the way we love things.

the word which is not a thing something we do. rather. threatens to become. since standing in the center nailed down forever, escaping breath, or victim of fire, any holocaust, catastrophe, what will endure. the word itself is a catastrophe, its sign.

its sign. something happened. turning another way.

—

if I don't call you it's because I forgot. selected bits and pieces. now it's summer again, though fading fast. how time flies. how it has wings, an 8 foot wing span, and steals from the gulls. how among the cactus they work out time. the boobies. the flightless cormorants.

two and then there's no end of it. the train to Palo Alto its hum comes back in a line. visible, what is heard, what is joined. it echoes in the landscape but a painting exists in silence. a photograph also more so. what is time that speech structures it that space is empty that words in space are empty but words in time are speech are time.

the growling weather the insatiable fox the break into the open. tangential. or transcendental. rising above it. they go straight up like smoke. I would have liked to hear how it came out, but she was in no mood to call me. we were not that far from home. not that far from what had been given. there was always the sense behind it of the one-noted train, calling. in childhood the train was an animal.

following that she dropped from sight. follow the thought, it goes some-where. in narrative we follow a trail, the clues laid out. that's how it becomes the illusion of space. that we follow it. the ubiquitous Galápagos trail marker, the post painted black and white.

we know this is a piece of writing. we condense the time. it really took much longer. there is no real time in writing. no 'total reading.' language is an after thought.

she got off the train. mumble, mumble, "off to get cigarettes in the sad foggy

San Francisco night" we parrot, laughing, I'm washing dishes in the pine cupboard pantry, summertime, we live constantly at the beach. yes, always live at the beach, and I do, where else, half the world must be homesick.

homesick. what is 'homelike' becomes 'unhomelike.' or think what has happened to our word *homely*.

a cup like a piece of granite, rock that rock, that held it, the stone holding it, that may even have been its source.

the source split, who plunged his sword in the rock, out gushed water.

how long it took to recognize it how many hours or days until it was finally established as a memory. until it sank out of time out of mind. sank to the bottom the silt filling up. how soon it happens that the crocodiles come back. how quickly that something is growing again on that barren stretch of land. how no sooner had it cooled than something was growing on it, some fern, some moss.

tough, tough enough, that looked fragile. what is a repulsive idea? what would I think that I wouldn't think? what would I think without claiming it?

unsettling. that was the third wound. to know someone was stirring up the depths.

parallel time and then the music begins. it ties up the space. that tying into the chair wherever I had seen that before, had also done it, a tying like music, her words like knots in the rope. time the knots. the twist of the noose. the hangman, the stretched bodies. the child Ezra who is already storing that up. childrening it.

—

lay under the heat, turning to it, the filthy sky. lay with the ribs exposed, she took the bones, painted them, the loss, turned that to art, and still they were bones, the dead animal. fails to save. the world spinning out of shape.

all this flies away and is lost on us. the story of the white deer at dusk which I could not see and could not tell, then saw, or thought I saw, the faintest glimmer. the others had seen it, they convinced me. they went to Europe to see what the others had seen, they saw nothing new, nothing for themselves. sitting in that room, recounting maps and castles. my mother feigned interest. feed me. feed me. everything is hungry. stuffed. hummingbird at the window, the *tut tut tut* of the robin. out of the thrush. a disease, a secret organization.

whanging, dense heat, the puppy begins whining again. *Halloa*, they say in old novels, the sounds of the vowels, the meat of the word. the rigid formality of the speech of Mr. Sherlock Holmes. I am no nearer to you now than I was at the beginning. this little garden under glass bound like the foot of the Chinese woman.

I am no nearer to you than I was before. these are words, one at a time. a step. one at a time. learning to walk, I fell down the backstairs, skinning my nose.

an assortment, a variety, that explosion of flowers he spoke of, remarkable, and the wings of the butterfly with patches of silver. why do it? fish flashing in the depths, what is it for.

a fallen woman, amnesia about dreams, ringing ears, a stiff back. the sun aslant in a patch on the bed. I said to her, I don't think you understood me, it wasn't in cans, it was curled up in a jar and grinning at you with all its teeth, like a laboratory specimen.

lost it, whatever it was, that deep speaking that may have been the names of the months: October, November, December; the hours painted in gold on the glass door of the bank, and in Spanish: *Lunes*, Monday. Moonday. Monday, Monday.

the scavengers prowling in their wide-hipped trucks, grinding.

no more, birds, clucking, a ring-necked pheasant, a China rooster. there, in the garden. hunger begins, a welling up, a ticking in the head that is both inside and outside, faintness, blending into a swoon. I can't tell you how happy I am. and the faint traces of the dream, hanging paintings.

—

the paper through the wringer. an advance.

the work changed. from fireplaces to wood-burning stoves.

the work. what work depending on time, the accidents of history, *accidents*, whatever is beyond us, our powers, the limitations catastrophe imposes.

then he asked me to read but I had none of my own work and was about to read a passage from *Two Years Before the Mast* but was interrupted by a child.

that unintentional music which the foghorns make, a calling that paces the morning.

I was interrupted by a child, I was oiling the wood, the wicker, all the furniture and fireplaces in her house while she was away, and taking care of her children, and finally turned sullen and rebelled. no thanks. how did I get there? she comes home in a sports car, the house stands alone in a field of wild grass. three storied, haunted, he wanted to be everybody else. fake. three stories. intertwined. the balloon mask.

pushing and pulling, the threads broken, the line going another way. the sky falling, chicken little, little bit, the one who planted the grain of wheat, said who will help me, the little red hen. Rhode Island reds, Rock Island line. the sky falling, broken, broken into, what if that were god, God, wherever that was, the bad clouds, the gray ones, raining.

they wanted to recreate the sense of home, in Minnesota, in Oregon, in the woods, near the ocean. finding a place that looked like home to them, when they found their mother's country. this home, which is not a fast car.

pulling it out, whatever it means to have a home, not a jail, a mother, taking care, split, I am partly my mother taking care. in a jam, a pickle, she was the source of language, breathing down my throat, she spotted it. mama the trickster, the knave. the fool. now shall the circle be unbroken. a wreath in the window at Christmas, the glazed pane, this day you shall be with me in paradise.

the incense went up, the black and the white, and mixed. outside they were looking for a sign. he had painted all the stop signs for three miles so that they read *stop the war* and was caught and got four years for it. four years for your trouble, your pain, and never a face, not to face the accuser, the father of lies is invisible.

she said those squash were called pitty-pats, and I couldn't remember any other name, yellow-bellied sapsucker, ornithology, the name of that tune, a puzzle, a test. I was looking for the hidden words and eventually found them, all of them. we were bringing the dog home in that game along a circuitous path. they built something in the center, a circle, a circus, and that was the place of the dance. sleepy-time gal, hello my honey, hello my kitty, hello my good-time girl. the songs I sing to the things around me, to the maidenhair fern, 'to think you were an orphan on Polk Street,' whimpering in the rain at the corner by the hardware store, a dog lost and beaten from cruel master to master, the pathos of childhood. come home now, there is a place for you at the table, the sun has gone down

> *Your spring & your day, are wasted in play*
> *And your winter and night in disguise.*

to think you were outcast on Polk Street, in this daily musical comedy, my head in the clouds, my Camera on Point Lobos. The Sky Clears, there never were such things as Indian love calls, that was all the fantasy of the white man. it was later they were infected by romantic love. a sense of loss. hard liquor and a sense of loss.

the savage mind, primitive, original, first things. putting first things first, when I am a man, in my father's house I must be about my father's work. what was my father's work that he put off, and so willed to me, they may be fathers of the flesh but the spirit is fathered

the spirit is a feather, a bird, rubbing my hands together in glee because he whistled the birdsong, then made speech of it, just as it's done in the field guide, the call of the quail supposed to be *Chi* ca *go Chi* ca *go*.

the field guide says the purple finch looks like 'a sparrow dipped in raspberry juice' but I had changed that. my memory of the line was 'a sparrow dipped in wine.'

—

the high and the low, I was sunk into that dream trying to recall it, like coffee, like a bowl of chocolate frosting. if I wander at Woolworth's, in that violence, trying on the masks, looking for something, what was it? sunk in it, mindless, hungry, filled up with the passing noise, a jointed skeleton, the day of the dead. the day of the dead, la, la, la, cheap candy to pacify the spirits, to trick them, she wrote: thought a hysterectomy was having the vagina sewn shut. his shut mouth, shut forever, that silence. and his sister wrote notes to him, and talked to him as he lay in his coffin, as if he could see or hear. the uncanny: as if the dead could see or hear, something beyond us, watching us.

—

what happens when you open your mouth and say what you don't believe, a Sunday school you, that speaks of the powers that be, because we have nothing in common, and yet I kneel beside her when she says she hears the wind, and she is clearly in the world we do share, for the first time since I have known her. the corn is sacred therefore, simply, it is between us, we have nothing else. she is an old, old woman, she imagines the wind, in that ear of dried corn she hears it.

our only hope would be bam bam bam, dipping into it, she said, toes in

—

the water, leaning towards it, the longhandled dipper. something like the Tarot figure, pouring water back and forth. these are rows, rows of corn, the kernels, the teeth in rows, that braiding called corn rows, that long strand of hair which I found could not have been my own. blonde Laura. how how jazzy. the hearing of it bears it out. a stringed instrument, lute or guitar, dulcimer, and the drum. and yet I would not argue, he said, that it was an organic form. because he ran through it, because they were words on the run, a chase, a flight, a fugue. in which one theme flies in the face of an other.

flying in my face, birds startle, fly up, a long stretch of geese flying, out in the open sky. my brother disguised as the snowman, blood on the saddle, and blood all around. he read: it rained all night the day I left, the weather it was dry. I said: she buys meat, and I buy milk and bread.

—

a building being wrecked, torn down, that theatre torn apart, the bare stage, mangled, walls gone, wrecking ball, a line in a poem of F.'s, wrecking the sky. balling the sky, the upward thrust, the spear of the narcissus, Narcissus anyway, the shadow, in those stories of de Angulo the people sing to their shadows in the morning, so that the shadows, which have been out travel- ing and seeing the world at night, will be able to find the people they belong to, because you cannot live without your shadow. and if that shadow were lost you must die. Egyptian & African shadow stories as well, and folks taking precautions against those who would steal the shadow. the theatre and its double, the ego and its double.

the point of those stories was to meet Coyote on the journey and to put the older stories into his mouth. so that he speaks from further back. there is a frame. in this journey we hear what used to be, who did what a long time ago, and they say that is the truth, it came down to us (wisdom being somewhere up there in the sky, the ascended events of the past), 'I didn't make it up myself!'

—

San Francisco & Palo Alto
June 18– November 3, 1978

Two

I sing of a maiden
'. . . German tree cults . . ?'

the celebration of that freeing of the bond, in nature, of conception and increase so that women might bear at any time in the year. a birth in the winter. that was the burden, the necessary burden, the import of the song, the argument of the play. in this way she made the advantage, delivered, birthed all year long, even in the dark. even so. even so, she died, and the children also, and none would have lived to tell the tale without her labor. her lot. our hollow mouths, mourning backwards, the ice on the trails, the blood on the ground, that little patch to which she was bound. no wonder no mouth, all breasts and belly, it is there by the rule of denial, devouring. the mouth is death, hell-mouth, *what have I to do with thee?*, she who pondered all these things silently.

rather the stars/*neaten the stars*/she was screaming and then *it's so unfair* she said. agreed, yes to that no, skin to skin, how that softness persists.

blank, it was a rule of thumb, black thumb, someone's new press, imprint, printer's ink. how could you call that a clock? it was winding, trailing, the shadows filling up the forest on a June evening, I was reading that, reading it with a falling for summer which is always long ago and far away. even in childhood it never came, it was a fairy tale, something to look back on. I cannot tell myself a straightforward story.

the crooked paths, or the woods without trails, she wrote how she followed her grandfather in the pathless woods, hunting, how a log became a crocodile, snakes in the water, how things became animals, enemies, enmity forever, my heel shall crush thee.

that was how I remembered it. how a senseless rock suddenly had eyes, the stupid world looking at you, it made a claim, had the prior claim, had been there longer, was not anything like you. except in the eyes.

you and I know the many reasons why these thoughts come crowding into the mind. they come in a crowd, in a swarm.

there is someone, that you in the first place, to whom these words are being spoken. they are part of the effort to heal my back. which was torn stooping. this was part of that effort, a war effort. but this is not literary, I said to him, and she isn't Proust, she has no memory, her mind is full of holes. she sees, god knows how, and speaks, but still there must be some language, a language I am trying to learn from her. I call it aphasia, what do I know. a word covers a multitude of emptiness, if that is not the void, what kind is this?

human language is not a code, it is something else in which we speak the third world, a world unconquered. where id was there I shall be, shall come to be, going there, as if it were another country. I would not be looking for it if I had not already found it. or: *I desired to desire thee*. falling in love again. her musky voice.

now *smoke gets in your eyes*, our light voices she told us, trying to prepare us for the sound of our own light voices after the deepness of the others. but we heard it and knew we were children. sang *Finlandia*, my grandfather in the audience, dear land of home. some mythical home in the old country, *somewhere I have never traveled gladly beyond*, or toward *where we will all meet again*. lay down a life for that, for the unbroken circle, for the promised land.

so long boys, I said, I'm on my way to California.

there is an other, she who is in the mirror, the many faces, none of them recognizably myself, the visible history of flesh, the chains of a family, that binding which is the only limit we know.

you, whoever it was, wherever there are two or three gathered together in my name. but she did not have a name for it. she said we could call it red if we wanted to, that would be all right, it would be a place to begin, but it wouldn't be the particular, not the exact thing that it was, there was no naming that, no word for it. she said it was highly worked. I thought she said it was highly worked. she spoke of the embroidery. that's what I had in my notes. but she was the one who said it, she was the one who said *that's what I seem to have in my notes*.

the red sand or the green in that sandbox, the roads, the towns we built, landscape with trees, the lumps of wet sand becoming a tunnel, a road, a place where the train went, where people walked, but there were no people. the miniature town, the pool, the tiny garden, a secret place.

a landscape, a wall, nothing, it refers to nothing but color, paint, the size and shape of the canvas, the way the paint is laid on, the thickness or thin-ness of the paint on the surface, the way it dried, shiny or dull, the quality of the reflection of light in the particular room where it was hung. that was all. except that it was pink. it was not empty of pink. it was full of pink. one might ask: why pink? this detail of pink. then there is language. hard to avoid the connotations of pink.

starting and stopping in the cold, moving from the bright side to the dark, out side in. now the sun shines on my back door. someday. whenever, as in graffiti. some of this is lost. *I remember, I remember* . . . but you were such good friends, mother said. a simple form, molded, but the possibility of infinite recurrence juxtaposed. a relation of pronouns. that's all. but he was wrong about so-called primitive languages, that they lacked grammar. a language is about relationship, that's what grammar does. it's a structure of relations. grammar prior to vocabulary. naming, what is the need to name unless there is something out there to name, realizing in that act that I am not this, that is other. me wants it. me wants to name what is lost, to cover the losses, to show (as in a play) by a word that it is gone, out there, no longer part of me. o language, the first and last sign of loss.

this word that was in the beginning was never no word and it wasn't the beginning. it was later. if there was a word for beginning, then it was later. if there was a body it became word. nobody thought you up. not you. not you. it is beyond your poor power to add or subtract. we are talking about a father who was already dead. this word was supposed to cover that. it would be a sign unto you. he was not dead forever but born again in the son. who also died. again. that is the grammar. the sign of the dead father is that his word lives. the word lives as if it were his body. that being so, words behave as bodies, beget children, are children, ghostly swarms and crowds.

the sign of the father. the sign of the lamb.

—

in the exchange nothing happens except that two people talk to one another. they crowd around.

this is the story of my life. I cast her in the third person or in the second person at will. who is this I? who asks the question already knows the answer. it is nothing, illusion, something made up out of loss, desire. you suffer her fate. she, and not he. the child is a gift and suffers the fatality of the given.

amnesia, it's amazing how much is forgotten. the analysis of a phobia forgotten in later years, the resistance to it, clearly against the reminders. everything, everything takes place, the generation of ideas, everything built on that shaky ground, everything covers it.

taking refuge in abstraction, so the content of the fantasy dissolves, becomes sheets of colored light. I told her yesterday that the holly symbolized the crown of thorns. he was a thorn in my side, we say, but that thorn was not witch shot. we needn't blame her for the trouble we have breathing.

there are tortuous elements, writing as an aid to memory, total recall. even she, however, had moments of amnesia. and the mirror writing which she performed so well, which became a little trick of hers, the double, the split.

but you were such good friends, mother said. the puffball.

OLLY-OLLY-OLEAAAA, OLLY—olly oxen free. beginning at twilight. I would never have written poetry. I was not interested in preserving the mysteries, I wanted to know why.

why is it forbidden, why is it concealed.

eyes, eyes in the dark, on strings, balloons, the balloon man chased me up the hill from Fanakis Grocery in that dream from childhood. that place of great light one was sworn to, a father ascended, radiant. the yellow roses, that's at the bottom of it, the twilit cherrytree shadows, the rustling of a poem.

that stretch of hill, fenced, the monkey tree grew there. catastrophes dissolve in a cloud. a cloud dispelled the darkness. I made the vow to it. I would not have treated you this way. I would not have treated you this way if I had known.

those were the eyes of my double, loose and crazy. I might never have known this except for the accidents of history. truth may be forbidden, might not be level as a desert.

the desert landscapes I drew, that place which I had never seen, always mountains in the distance. how anything might mean its opposite.

eyes, eyes, fierce and searching, disembodied, and yet not wholly. attached to something by strings, they were not yet completely alien. strings, strings, they might have been snakes, another version, blessed be the tie that binds, the cord, which later would choke me, waking in the morning, my hands around my neck, a schizophrenic episode. and yet in the demonstration years later, all who saw it said it was an act of protection. I had defended myself though I believed otherwise.

we do not yet know what it is we fear. the fear attaches itself to what is out there loose and crazy. that could be me. *I could be the wall. It is a terrible thing for a girl to be a wall.* we repeat it. it sticks in the mind. stuck there. that, out in the grass, was a part of myself, escaped from me, my baby, the malevolent child, deformed, I should not have thought this otherwise, I might never have known. that part of myself which might turn against me, that had seemed something other. fixed on it. fixed.

so he said the naming of the flowers which carries us back. carries us back and around. that naming of the flowers which carries us forward. and completes the circle, the figure. but the snake itself became a wreath in those figures of the eternal, was not simply or only nailed to the cross, the sign of the father and son, but was also the mother as a circle, the limit of what we are.

and so the child in his plunging. covers his losses. the alternation of generations. sending the father backwards. the two-timing father. out of that roses grew.

I would not have written poetry except for that opening. otherwise madness. in principle. Ferenczi's aphorism to that effect. the consciousness detaching itself, flying away. the purely phallicized body, so burned, I meant burdened. the course of that fantasy. *oh yet we trust that somehow good will be the final goal* etc., Freud's prayer to Eros at the end of his life, he who had stirred up the seamy side, naming and naming, it was not chaos, charted it. *and still she cries.*

how bound to our chains. the work of a lifetime. one by one unknotting that, taking it apart at night in order not to be trapped, suffering that fate, for ten years waiting. nothing to go on. no news. she might have been a pair of ragged claws. he in that poem, waiting, the way life waits before the invention of time. and then it all goes so fast. the forms we are charmed by. lost in them.

lost in it, the way we lose ourselves in our work, how can we recognize ourselves in it? the way God is lost in nature. nature as God's alienated labor. but we do not see it that way. nature is what is given, given to be transformed by labor. what of the relationship to the gift?

the gift signifies guilt, we are already caught up in it the moment we are born. bearing the guilt. it was not ours but we are born into history. it becomes ours. we cannot do otherwise. we cannot refuse it. Freud's prayer to Eros. there is nothing in the unconscious that corresponds to *no*.

—

San Francisco
November 18 – December 11, 1978

Three

this is the time of Advent and a time of waiting I told them. and a time of lighting the candles and wondering whether the sun will return.

in the tree of life there were many branches not the least among them the rabbits, the hat dance, the sliding scale, I was keeping up with you.

he said they had the sun every day of the year. I would somehow have the dream, the way it felt, without being able to lay hold of the image. I thought it was a kind of hemming in.

grant us another year, another part of the time. another part of the time another branch. another coming forth by day. that in the all in all.

she wrote that nobody really knew what this thing was but the person or god who made it. she had the idea that it might have been god-made. she noticed that it was a sacred vessel. it was an opening. it marked itself as an opening. for that reason. because it could contain something. it could hold it.

—

recognition and the annihilation of differences. we do not want anyone to be different from us. aphasia. seeing that whole categories of desire were wiped out. but mother said it was there, further back. she said you know how you go further back. she pointed to the back of her head. she said there you really did see it, as if in childhood one saw that blue and orange made brown, as if in childhood one saw the world discretely, there were the elements, one and one and one. further back, she said, we have that knowledge.

my mother the romantic. I didn't believe her. and yet I might have known. and she wondered why something could be so beautiful it would make you cry. she wondered if anyone else felt that way. I said yes. I said yes. there was a question I had been studying all my life.

do you see the star? a spider has already been working in it, mother said. I said I thought it was a strand of angel hair left over from years ago. Christmases ago. ago. ago. and yet the birds were still there. not the same birds surely. that *identity of nature with itself* invisible. going on in the background. who sees it. who walks to the river and hears the song of the golden-crowned sparrow. it is difficult to account for, even where the name itself is not lost.

—

a new year, looking both ways, she crosses the street. the light against me, in my eyes. looking up, squinting. taking pictures inside the womb, he said, is nothing sacred? but I was just a child. here the thought broke off. and yet I was aware of the connection, the father, the sun. the father, the son. my own brother, the little sadist. I cursed him. he laughed.

and yet I was feeling a tenderness towards things, towards myself. every each thing, that seemed to be a gift. enough, mother said, to take care of all Asia.

it comes this way, *he came all so still where his mother was*, he comes in the sense of rain, in the spring, then he comes. he might have been a son of mine, or myself as the son. these names in contradiction and yet there is nothing in the unconscious which corresponds to *no*. one will be the all in all. I will sing you one-o.

singing
the day at an end
the dark shadows of January
waiting, the dark days of December
and January

—

still one must invoke the other somehow, to whom one speaks, that other who bears the burden, lightly, my yoke is easy, in the marriage ceremony they were yoked together. having undertaken this work, this labor. he who is other must be the final mystery, who lives under the law of the dead father. but I do not know him. I who live so much outside the law, as all women do. with my *impaired moral responsibility*.

the slights and injuries. there was another code, another order, a counter order, the question of loving strange women, why that should be necessary, universally, the necessity of loving strange women.

our own work, each one has made a change for the better, never lifting pen from paper. remembering the orders, only long enough to take a sip of coffee, Willits, or someplace in the mountains, coming in from the bus on a cold day, drinking coffee at the counter. somewhere in the mountains, a real pine lodge, snowing outside, fire in the big stone fireplace, that story about T. freezing in the only snow, the peach, the simile of the cock and the peach, lovely, yes, of course. peeling the peach that day, S. noticed it, everything speaks.

there is something, a world we call it. the blue morning glory, the porcelain tea set. how beauty as a mark of life, why should it be there, that it takes place, but I would not have been a poet since there is no beauty in language because we do not love words the way we love things. I tell you this and you will know the reason why. I am filled with unspeakable pleasure.

—

on a day in winter how wonderfully and darkly the vines cling to the fence, rise around the pole, how darkly stand forth among the wet fence boards, the deep colors, the dark and mossy, the graying, the only yellow in lowly-ing patches and thickets of willows, the deep, the rusty life of the willows, where did I see those colors? walking by the American River on Christmas Day.

where, I thought, my own tenderness towards things, privileged, I thought, I am privileged to walk beside the ocean at Epiphany, the surf white in the lowlying dusk, a line of pink, a strip, a bar, a patch of sky between the clouds going out at sunset, going out a grayed yellow, it is that, a strain of light, winter light, a winter's tale. not metallic, not the brooding wings, the washing, the ablution, the purification, resisting the ceremony, or any words to fix it.

there is a bare stripped-down quality about it which is its true subject. unquote. release those lines into the air.

it would be nice, she said, if you would take this patch of blue and make something of it. as he had said it was time to make something of yourself. making something, scratches and doodles, people will look at it, they will have an appetite for such things, they will develop a taste for quiche, for albatross, for moldy bread. they will go by threes. they will march in the streets protesting. they will rise up children and follow.

in that arc, that flash from a long way off, she followed it. the detail was lost, scrubbed out, she noticed how the darker windows appeared at first glance to be columns of smoke rising from a line of factory chimneys when the sky was a certain color, a grayed white in which the walls of the building were lost, disappeared. then she remembered. there were no factories there. she wondered why she was taken in by that illusion every time. ordinarily the sky was blue. yes, it was a photograph of Toledo, she recognized it from the painting by El Greco.

we were living in the present time and did not want to be disturbed by illuminations from the past.

the continuity had been shattered; she wondered why it had turned out this way. why in the world, expecting the end of it, it would continue, coming true. one would reach a high and level plain, signaling the others, who were still below, that it was there, such as some, but not all, old maps had predicted. the broad outlines were there, but not the details. it looks, he said, a lot like it looks on this side.

—

San Francisco
December 22, 1978–January 7, 1979

Four

same in here and yet not the same
losing its leaves and flowers
organically
maybe
the wretched or wrenched
the quicksilver
it flows in the dark street on the waterfront

clearing that erased it with a movement of the hand on the machine
it was blue
a rather bright a bright blue
caught in a shock from that blue to the eyes
comforting the boards laid out their innards
it stepped on toes got in the way looked to see what damage
sign a single word in reference to a billboard
she was our mother she knew it everyone knew it she was pictured
that way a mountain a mountain the sculpture hewn
she had no children was mother to
right into the night walking in complex air
that was a single weaving wove dedicated the strands
father's face
out in the garden walking walking around
deer come here sheep crossing
the low and long hills
the spurious investigation
scrubbing his skin washing washing
distracted a cat
farming giving it elbow room egg
it moves up as a piece of sculpture white a world
no way to touch that except to touch it
abandonment
as mean as they were one to another
but I wanted to come in his arms
the range of possibilities the range that was the word
threw the carriage back
the horse reared

jumping the face jumped it was blue on the screen
filling o I had been filled the yellow bucket he squatted and
nodded to the filling water

—

under it there are some vague gray or black shapes, boxes, their lids flapping
open, hanging there. they glow. she was in every state, her portrait, her face.
the music was on top of it, the tune circulating, went, nailing down very
softly, one mockingly dangerous place in it, so that it satisfied every need in
a very simple way for a long time.

there are some plugs like organ stops which are pushed in and everything
else is going strong. the music honks and it takes up everything, it is a meal
in itself.

go put that together. it doesn't easily turn around. it doesn't easily. it doesn't
go in. not easily. it remains not going in. it stays there in that very simple
place, just going over and over it, over the same ground; what very simple
activities filled our lives, we don't outgrow it.

—

throwing that in a heap they clang out.
a noise gets smaller.
the eyes meet somewhere.
there is a surface and not an edge.
this is the way it is done. I will tell you about it.
it will take longer to tell about it than to do it.
then there is the reading and the source for it.
then we will see how the words stick together and try to take them
apart.

wrong with it, I hear it and I am trying to
trying to listen
going off alone on a boat, a raft like Huck and Jim
since this part was story telling
trying to figure out the plot inventing it
plots within plots the mind of a mnemonist
the cause
walking down the street a simple procedure

everything in a line.
going backwards but this was when you had to look both ways
at once. happy new year.
and he made up the story about the river which was already the
oldest story in the world.
from such simple beginnings we might get lost.
nothing is known nothing is what it seems to be

—

bitterly the coffee
a round
a round tasting that lights up the mouth with a whole definition
a creamy darkness

stopping on the word it turns around roars in your face
that's what he meant
I don't know what he meant I mean it roars at you.
it was not following you
that mis-remembering
you were following it as usual.
it was ahead of you. as it always was and you knew that
but did not recognize it.

catching up walking quietly behind it
it hunches is angry but not hungry
scared but not scarier than

tracking it. already at the beginning.

—

nothing interferes with it, walking around with rags on his head,
contraptions, wires of bells, thistles.

this sensorium, aquarium or indoor garden.
rare birds.

the way it jumps around was never such a source
pinned
floating on top like garbage
wisely

dog	lowering motor
one bark	bus
medium far away	down the hill

tik tik tik tik tik tik tik tik tik tik tik tik tik tik tik tik tik tik tik tik tik tik tik

dim purple	really the cat	blah of water
winding hum	sharp short	next door
other cars	screech	hose bang into
		garbage can

tik tik tik tik tik tik tik tik tik tik tik tik tik tik tik tik tik tik tik tik tik tik tik

etcetera the world
going on
the clock a continuo
ground bass
to what happens on top of it

—

it goes on you can't look at it
for fear of injury blindness
trying to see it out of the corner of an eye
a room, *cirrus can barely get under the door*
he said and I laughed
he knows so much we don't have a leg to stand on.
what if knowing what if a kind of green
serious older
what if older
getting the religion mixed up with the language
I labored
I had not been working here very long
a short time ago
when bottles
sea green bottles
and the smoke inside
I said I thought it was trapped
some small animal
closer to animal
and the smooth bodies of women
women. women how they
love it such an expansiveness of flesh
such lovely breasts ridges

no wonder the gorgeous bones *that thing*
which it is and no other thing
the filtered light
I thought o god touch touch touch
lover her in the palm of my hand
in my very only body
that line that hill that was me
I can barely believe turning bodies into art
how they long for it skinny flaming
licked up in it sucking his cock seasalt
the hair
holes eyes all air and curling

—

San Francisco
February 4-26, 1979

Five

partly nightmare, weakness, succumbing. we walked down the steps. I said I
don't want to do this, walking in at hell-mouth, why, to separate myself to
be underground gone

to be gone for a while tasting that again

and he
he who was
a figure of the god
Dionysus
hidden in the side of his father

> on me again the drunkenness I went through it
> bent my head to it yielding *the gift of bearing*
> he wrote, my hands in that effort to hold on to
> it, not moving I went through it, it took me,
> carried away by it, taken, overtaken, I had come

to this place, it was made for me, I fitted into it, I knew
what place it was

it was hell and I walked down the steps
bearing.

he who was also torn apart, the women in the wilderness tearing, outside the law, they would have it, devour, that mouth.

and the wine which was on me. *the gift of bearing*. he who had borne it, not to be stopped. I had not known his name, I had not known it, he who was hidden in the side of his father, and then we were already walking down the steps, I did not want to go on that rescue mission, a mother to be rescued, there in the arms of death, a mother seeking sought, in the underworld, going down there.

I was looking for a god. I already knew it. how

> getting off the bus on Valencia Street
> some night and walking into the arms
> of an old friend do you expect to
> see it, sitting in some funky taco place
> Eros all over me, silly, I wouldn't
> see it, his wild

beard and hair
some secret mission
some place in the mountains to get to
some way going
how should I know

speaking in tongues I gave him all the time he needed to get out of my life. Get out.

it had come to this. and then he picked up the harp and blew. blues. how I would not mother him, sister him, be any

other or none, nothing to do with it, forsaking it
what I had given up forever how soon would it bring me lead me

down those steps
he where I would see him

in those stories they never recognize the god. and then it's too late.

—

a feminine ending. clarity. the moon on stark hills.
the one damn thing. the one damn thing I meant to do.

negative. throw down the cards. negative. a negative throw. what you tell
anyone, skimming the surface. what, getting down to it, you really would
say, that he was a home boy, one counted on that, homing instincts. the
domestic male. . . . *would be a house dove roosting in the trees and eating the
mast were he not wild.*

how did I come to love that? she who had so much contempt for it. how
did I come to love that sturdy gaze, that garden rose, that inclined plane?
how in the face of adversity.

how every finding, fiinding again, remembering the dead body, the scattered
other, his parts, how she wept from town to town, how all those women,
Isis, Psyche, Mary, holding the dead cock, what life after this one? what possible, what birth of tragedy, Erzulie, what mother of us all, weeping, inconsolable, that dear heart, these lovers, gone, sons, always some mother's son.
every last mother's son of you.

—

trails, a certain path, a road.

a father, this was his part I was playing, to say yes to all that unclaimed
wilderness, that territory he would have struck out for, leaving us, leaving if
he hadn't loved us, hadn't made the sacrifice to that love. I myself an agent,

Daddy, mom wants you to come home now, and he bending and turning, he came, came with me, back. such a man. and I a child learning the woman's part, come home now. be civilized, this is the order, we have made it, we have made these exchanges, this for that, lay it on the line.

but I loved wild men. the sorrow of my life. who also wanted. not to cancel out.

—

ah the onomatopoeia. palindrome. excess. same backwards and forwards. upside down. turning the world upside down, he was threatened with it. he who was also a she. Tiresias. alliteration. a sameness at the beginning.

what goes on in there, mundane thoughts, it hit me like a ton of bricks, not that again. driving by, he said the road of excess leads past the palace of wisdom, right over the cliff on the other side, I said. falling. he thought of a fall through space. my own fall was less drastic. a fall from grace. or into. falling in love again. that way lies madness.

this dumb day, rainy, exhausted. a subliminal war going on. he said it was a conspiracy against us to rob us of our sleep. among garbage men. I said whatever happened to my old poverty stricken friend, best scavenger in this neck of the woods. these literal conversations.

I suspected he was getting by with a lot. glowing body, dripping sweat. there was some backwater I was in, couldn't get out of it. some slough where I put myself on again, these clothes.

now you might put your foot down anywhere and not know.

pulling at some lower
sound inarticulate
gut mid-level gut

uh
u   au   ojshh

these smallest particles of meaningful
research
let me ask you
how come you do

no tears. not canary. imbecile. weather.

he was a rationalist, suspected her of play, was right, she was, hadn't any
idea what she was doing, did it. playing. drawing the veil over the more
serious business. what is the more serious business? there is someone else
out there, someone who really is another. not oneself. we cannot abide
it/will not take no for an answer. the burden of difference.

she said you go there and then you make the map. there aren't any maps,
every journey into the wilderness, Sacajawea appears, we go over the mountains, find our way to the ocean, 'oh the joy.'

that place a carnival now, sideshows, this play taking the place of. that
break through the trees. and this is how it turned out. 'what child is this?'
little America.

I thought of those gates, one after the other, closing. that finality.

here the trail diverges.

Medea, 'ask what desperation drove her to kill what she loved most,'
that question.

her mind gone, gone to the racetrack, this wind, gone with it. the mini,
mini, mini-Ophir, trees in bloom, molly, mother. babies. eternal angels.
in this room there are angels, there are crackerjacks, marbles and pins.

forever a book that we loved. because we were trying to find out which
story it was, what we were playing now. so and so many roles, so many
pieces of meat, so many birds. I was shocked by that.

guarded. the *uuuuuuuuuuuuuuuuuuuuuuuuuu*.
u, the, *u,* pieces of blood
            u, u, u, u, u
failure, the blood,
            one's life, one's life, one's life
a life, what and how with
      would
you and then the blood
this is a meditation on Medea

seeing that she was any woman a slave an exile
seeing that her power was nothing to him
nothing nothing it kills
nothing it kills
nothing will always kill
nothing will turn around and kill you
nothing this emptiness kills
nothing she is nothing nothing she was nothing to him a hole
bones
her bare head
think how she loved him think of it
think of her slavery the temptation of slavery
think of submission how everything still says slave slave
your calling your perfection
no other life
her devotion to slavery she would do it perfectly
think of it you have never known such devotion
never

she would say to him: worry, you worry that I'm traipsing around alone at
night in flaky neighborhoods, now you worry, now that you have a proprie-
tary interest in me, you never worried before, I've been doing this for years,

and you never worried before. it's sweet of you darling to worry about me
but you never worried before. you never worried about women. about a
woman, some woman, any woman you may have been attached to, but not
about women. not about women walking alone at night in flaky neighborhoods. why it happens. why anything happens because one is a woman.
from that day to this. and this is a part of our slavery, our exile, in which we
continue. in which, even now, we cherish the illusion that some man

will define
a life

and I resist it, you, the law of the father, who chose from among the
women, the slaves, who she would be, her children his, that she would take
that back, take that back all the way to death, claiming whatever she could
claim, a final power, all that she had. left. no ambiguity. nothing. nothing
left but to think of the knife. then she will. then she will make her claim.
then she will claim it. knowing what she is, then she will claim it. she will
claim what she is. nothing. she will claim it. she will claim that with all the
power she has left. she will pick up a knife and claim it.

—

I don't know.

I don't know where it will end, where the evergreen, forest,
bears lumbering.

I don't know, one thing follows another, and time stands still.

I don't know, my heart leaps up when I behold a rainbow in the sky.

I don't know, I have this ache, this gone, this bone in the head.

I don't know, look at the ground, the floor, look away. I wish
I were in Dixie.

wish nothing between us, no gap, gaping: 'wholeness, harmony, clarity.' wish that shine forth, forward, see it there, suddenly, what tears are these, 'whatsoever is grave and constant in human sufferings.'

I would not have been a poet.

what am I counting, what is certain, what would I countenance, what turn to face. a light. knowing what she was, how she brought children out of that, how deeply to sacrifice a life, to bring a child to a man, for him, to that altar, year in and year out, strange gods, captive women, captivity so deep, complete, we do not remember it and then we begin to remember, to take back the children, ours anyway, taking them back.

—

yes, of course, I have invented it.

but there were others, watching us. what did they see? I call them out of the darkness, truly. dark words turning to face. he is the hieroglyph for *n*. I don't know what that means.

spare me this. let this cup pass from me. I would not have been a poet. let this world pass away, in flames, let another take its place.

harbor me, let the lower lights be burning. imagining love: that great feat. Persephone returning, casting off her dark hair, her weeds. 'beautiful white corpse of night actually.' Hecate, Diana of the crossroads, Artemis. 'the only boy she ever loved was a boy disguised as a girl.'

then we came to a city of the dead. Osiris with an erection. sit on it. this brother, this sister. little brother, how can I not tell these stories about you. my life had become all a story, it would not answer. one is in the presence of powers, the appearance of the god is never what one expects, he is nothing but the most ordinary fellow. his opposite even, perhaps ugly, a toad, some animal, beast. that which sees is truly seen. under a cloud.

there isn't any last word you aren't having an argument nobody wins.

what would you trust? the goddamn politics. anybody trying not to be a slave. kiss me. what does it mean, kiss me. what does it mean, real, relative, relative to what, what relation. if you go off in space I am alone.

watching him arrange the flowers: dark stemmed iris, the blue flag, everything speaking, not a word, where does language end? what limits? an idea whose time had come, for that he got a bullet in the head. the relationship. the revelation of structure. don't ask. don't ask what you can do for your country.

love, what is it, under late high capitalism, under gas bills, armor, slaughter, what is it. a lyric episode, an inarticulate babbling, not one word in the whole lot. deconstruct that. go deconstruct that language.

this was a kind of writing. of speech. tonguing. how could he say how wrong that was? because words take the place of another, pretend, the violence of the word intervening. blessed or damned. 'no book ever ruined a girl's life?' I don't believe it. books ruined my life. my life is a ruin of books. I would give it up forever, go catatonic. and still there is a language. it is given, damn it, given, eat it. it's the same thing, overthrow it, if you love him go to him, what is it? what is love? what do we know?

illusion, fooling, lay a finger there. the great out? what do I know that I don't know, what metaphor, analog, did you think there was something hidden, that you could rend the veil, with what? words? the violence of the word. or words themselves as the veil, in this myth, bride and groom. he takes her, he rends the veil, the hair, her blood on his cock. *this is not nature* I told him, is this a language? Thalassa, the regressive trend. wholeness, harmony, clarity. this thing that it is and no other thing, light that, the light on those bones, skin, what knows, what mind, the double is with us till we die, we cannot live without her, it, him, whoever, they multiply, she is my mother, you too, you were my brother, but my mother's body, having that, to sleep with/against, her side, yours, by your side, waking in the night she was there. I don't think about it. there aren't any dreams. the regressive trend, the death in it, it is all we have. it is all we have left.

so they want a revolution. the furthest back one. to overthrow language, not language, the idea, something, what to smash, what to know so well you can smash it, knowing it was never yours, to take a step, to claim it in the beginning, he who was outside me, an other one. 'so there are at least three.' at the very least. is that a violence. or what we have. hallucination. 'I'm a noun.'

'no one.'

—

a place in nature. a truck roars. hand to key transcribing.

distraction, an ode.

the immortality ode, to my socks. Neruda, all the 'wonderful poets of this century,' all the crap, spit and fire, gum, hustling, street talk, organization, the proletariat, making it, inventing ourselves. going along.

I would not have been a poet, I wonder why that recurs, I wonder why I don't think about it, the key. a resistance. key, Freud knew that even without the censor there would be symbolism. we cannot speak directly as in nature, we speak, nature never does, the animal that makes symbols, toolmaster, weaver, orgone. the man who discovers her hidden in a tree is

not a natural animal, 'nature which is forever identical with itself,' therefore I wanted to shake him out of his sleep, we are not there, we are not where you think we are, that state of grace we abandoned, had to, driven from it, the gates closed behind us forever. off across what oceans of transformation, in these days history moves quickly, moves us along, the slave text, the master text.

miniaturizing those circuits so now we are inscribed with a new space. this is it. I came in that door. grown both large and small, into the garden. the garden who was a mother as the Queen of Hearts. vicious. what would a real girl find in that garden. really Alice beyond the Oedipal crisis. not in a tree, treed. leftover. we love her because she's he and because she has so much common sense, because she knows it is a dream. the quest for the historical anything it is all a screen memory. it never happened. how do they say? 'this is who they say she was.' the romantic love of ruins.

and the simple story of the plot, 'when considering text-sound it is energy,' delight, the pain and contradiction of the primal unity.

today we take as our text whether this world is saved or no, and at what moment in historical time, whether he comes again, but I said no to that, I don't believe, I said, in the eternality of anything, not even the unconscious. that lowest level of rap. in the unconscious nothing corresponds to 'no' and we move among those heights. a state of grace is unbidden, you may as well call it nature, you might as well be spring. dew in April.

after *The Psychopathology of Everyday Life* no one could ignore those mistakes, those little irruptions. a little insanity goes a long way, a lot of small earthquakes in order to avoid the big one, we are trying to avoid a theory of catastrophe. *deus ex machina*. he will descend. daddy. ok kids it's all over. go to bed. rabbits dance at four o'clock in the morning. if there is any benevolence in the universe it is human, taming that wildness, making a park, the lion and the lamb.

living according to our own lights, one law is oppression, I dreamed I was too slow, why.

shattered. what enters this house. bow down. an immense photograph of myself as a child, that unity, congruity, screen memory, living in several times at once, these were the conditions of life now. raising the flag on Iwo Jima, an image, a mythology. the uses of photography. the uses of the past. Garbo's face. her many faces. the icon. but walking in Greenwich Village, 'I want to be alone,' dark glasses, a woman of character, older, the eternal moment subverted. women subverting that, she is not here, she is risen as she said.

whom seek ye, she is not here.

—

if there was a question about the ending certainly there was also one about the beginning, where is the first word. at what point cutting or dipping, the big bang or the steady state.

theories of catastrophe. trauma. in response to that suffering, ice, the ages. now seen, unknown.

listening for it, waiting for it, what has been forgotten, expunged from the record, and yet there were witnesses. she testifies to it, what I can no longer remember, never forgot it, she said, broken, incoherent, she held me, who could have done this to me? evidently I have lived through it, mute scars, I can no longer find them, remember them. no I said.

it is true that we have lived through the end. everything on the other side is heaven. this *no* in which I prepared a limit. something within which, asylum.

bereft of home, ties, neither kith nor kin, the invention of a way to live there, we were not sure why we renounced it, or were renounced by it, instinctual renunciation. that trap. to home, going, that verb. it is not a person place or thing.

from thence. the ice. glaciation. ages and ages of it. the monster on the ice. on the rocks. a breathing in the dark.

light on the wood my mother's table.
I am on this side of it and then I see it as a microscope.
not "as a primary instance of 'language-oriented' writing."

all this has become you. who is this you. this other I address, the relation-ship of pronouns. he said on the one hand the history of the imagination and on the other the history of the self. we never talk about the subject, everything object, hard, a trajectory, what do these figures represent. if recurrence is not a theme they will not enter. is it possible that everything happens only once and never again?

disseminate the books, the reading lists. skim. insemination, this semen, taking this phallus, it was a book, all my life the books I have carried in my arms, cradled, I carry books, you carry babies. male mothers, the birth of books, the battles of ideas, a war among powers.

an achieved form, 'a form can be used once only.' how to classify, order things, this goes with that on account of X. rhyme scheme such and such, this rhymes with that, he said, looking back through the pages.

formally bent. angular. all my bones showing. I was not a showoff, I was going around the corner. around the bend, these psychotic breaks. that, a history of the self.

teaching in that way the mask of the poem believing those forms taken in by the masks, though I knew otherwise. the mask of my mother in the hospital, she believed she was she, utterly identified with her own face, nothing between them. my father's face that I thought I could lift and peel.

cant making words go. a speech act. happens. faster. than. then taking pictures at the speed of speech. light catching up. so the other, the mirror, however we know we aren't there except as. objects for another. o, she could blow the world away, a puff of dandelion smoke. I deliver myself. away from that. the years harden. tough language. some springing free.

if along here, dropping out. to be subject. why did I want all the articles in, all the *these* and *the* and *that*. pointers, another fiction, the moving finger pointing. pretending to point. a real little world, speech the speech act, the language act, discerning there beyond that curtain, we dance for, without the words I will be naked. I never wanted to wear those clothes, wearing them not knowing how to act in them, wrong wrong.

not thought clothed, old metaphor, but illusion itself, the play of it, maya, aurora borealis, the show deeply in muscles, tissues, down to it, we read you, an I, ego, through it, the medium.

Oppen: *Words cannot be wholly transparent. And that is the 'heartlessness' of words.*

making, as we say, love, 'good exercise, it strengthens the heart,' casting aside clothes, take off, but not the maya of words, gates, picking the locks, this rhymes with that, what is a rhyme but recurrence, doing it again.

hard to say, choosing, the binary nature of language, yes and no.

the skin was a kind of afraid. it was only the excitement before shitting.

fragment of an analysis of a case of wisteria. a word lightens a word. both words, we live them. why do I say we.

portmanteau. take care of the sounds and the sense will take care of itself. advice from the Duchess. everyone advises her. cuckoo adults.

wishing someone would give a talk against psychoanalysis in order to test, what, faith, embarrassing word, what is the ground of what you believe. how come it's easier to write her, that third person. how come saying I means I. a confession. the I is never identical with the fictional character being written. 'the moment of writing.' but what I that is not a fiction, there isn't one, me from moment to moment, I think I know where I am. 'where you are there arises a place.' a theory of relativity.

I don't understand it owing our existence to the black sky. if there were no night sky we would not be here in that rush away from the center. the universe moves out and away from us, Nut rises from the body of Geb, space is born, what do these figures represent. 'all gods reside in the human breast.' the figure of man only a few years old, 'it is good . . . to believe that the nation is only five minutes old, with time out for coffee.'

the red shift, everything is moving away from everything else, and flows in one direction, is irreversible. a disordered state, a running down. *Disappearing Work*. catch as catch can.

off star chasing, some sort of proof, news, that there are no limits. a Dionysian universe. a hole in the ground, a hole in space. there is no *I* there, the fictional center of things, no 'preferred observer.' it will look like that wherever you stand, where you stand you will be a center with everything rushing away.

if the sky were clear. if there were a bright blue line. a clear sense of horizon. that line we needed for, what was it she said? the health of the eye? blue eyes. look at all the blue eyes, she said, two and two and two around the table. recessive genes. bury me. 'Look for the blue-eyed Indian.'

I had to keep reminding myself that nothing he said in that work should be taken as identical with himself. not persona, against 'personality.' a deconstruction not of language but of ego. not identified with it, that mythical character. or that one could represent something, a part for the whole. a question about the 'authority' of language, what one believes through it, the unconscious is collective anyway. a reason for the anonymity, no name, that branch of mind, trading it in.

epistemology, from what proceeding. 'Is desire not that which remains always *unthought* at the heart of thought?' (Foucault)

an unthinking about it. stirring around. mother said she was up early stirring around. a rustling of taffeta dresses. we heard the water run. not knowing the origin, we had been cast up here. hunting backwards for the bases of that, the foundations of desire, why that 'style', the unconscious drift towards, something that looked like, vaguely, something in a photograph, it represented. an identity. the work of art in an age of mechanical reproduction.

was representation the long sleep from which waking. that stuffy world of the mirror. regressive, the flying into mirrors.

forking paths, and in some of those versions I am your enemy.

in a former life, in the back of your back, a book. somehow. text-sound. a noise made by women. to reiterate. she spoke. those sounds in the air. gone up like smoke. nothing saved.

writing scared, running with it.

whatever you choose, desire unspoken. finery. weapons.

endlessly in that place. Foucault: 'Henceforth, language was to grow with no point of departure, no end, and no promise. It is the traversal of this futile yet fundamental space that the text of literature traces from day to day.'

I could cry salty tears.

—

in the fullness of time. time, that virgin.

a fortune cookie with a blank message. a fortune cookie: a melon on the rooftop can roll either way. a fortune cookie. break it and read it. we smile. good friends, long life, and prosperity. what anyone wanted. anyone, she said, had become her favorite pronoun. these words standing in. the second team. a relief pitcher.

what's going on in there. direction, a scattering of genes, hit or miss. it doesn't seem likely, it seems highly improbably. but how quickly life begins there in that rubble. that inhospitable lava flow. one bush growing in that twisted wreck. weeds. overcompensation. life, in the midst of it.

you go out from yourself but the door is only the way in. a room is a life. or a lie. the light had changed and was no longer falling. why do we say it falls. when it seems to be everywhere not falling but floating. the ambiance. suddenly that plant was in bloom. when I had been waiting for it to bloom for over a year, suddenly one day it bloomed. it took me by surprise, by storm. I didn't notice it. I had no idea when it happened. she looked at me and frowned and turned down her mouth. she said it was all in my mind. what do I know that I don't know. something is moving profoundly in another direction.

good Friday riding westward why do they call that day good. why call it so, by any other name. ' . . . would be a house dove.' the rings. a fleeting image, a band, a pair of rings. how it was done. in the old days. I told her I tried to forget every word as I dropped it but a language is tough it persists. an echo hums, closing in, pursuing it, the sound. a certain. a beat of the word. wings. back and forth. from left to right by hand, she had, I said, an indecipherable hand. not the formality of the machine. this hand directly. the materials had changed.

in that it would grow dark.

I would not pursue it, the soil. worn out, down, 'her physical masterpieces.' a jewel of a lady. *A thought is the bride of what thinking.*

fish, that was his sign, a water dog. her list included salamander. my own orifice. office, the stations of the cross. a ritual of initiation. how could I know what was being said. line and line and line. scribble. this blue pen. contrary to popular opinion.

sending it off they all said goodbye. we stood around in the driveway and waved. then the car pulled slowly away down the street. we were still waving. some deaths, some so fast no time left to forgive.

—

who knows what it is, who knows it has a mind of its own. hard to think inhabiting it. 'I seem to be inhabity by imbecile dwarves.'

reading a mind, you can't do it. blank a mind. what is it, where does it live, in all the cells doing. it does. light. nothing miasma. it blocks out, blanks. doing whatever it does in the dark.

if you didn't know it how could you say how much it would change. a life. or two. you all. all of you are out there working on top of it. as if it weren't there in the dark. face this with me. face it. we must come to live in something like the same world.

I would not have cut down that tree, I would not have spoiled this child. she. I hadn't thought of her. he said she. yes.

what this yes means. the binary. symmetry. open-ended. the limits of yes. the limits of no.

baby, baby. crowning.

—

a new moon, a bowl of jelly. green. my mother's table, the tabula, the wax doll. voodoo. wouldn't you. I have no other heart. this was it. you don't get a second chance. dance, she said, you ought to dance. dance with me. all gone.

anything may mean its opposite, green may mean red, you can't tell an omen when you see one. reading it. must we go on reading as if we lived in the sixteenth century.

(All this language is floating. The men make statements. They use the forms of the verb 'to be' with confidence. What I write is provisional. It depends. It is subject to constant modification. It depends.)

(Equivalence.)

(They are so sure this equals that. Reading their sums.)

on the other hand. all dark. blank. the blank wall waiting. in it. waiting for something, The Other.

she who is absolutely other coming out of the dark. myself as the dark. in the dark. watching in silence the shadows. alone. it is given. giving with one hand and taking away with the other. they had decided to cut down the pine tree. no one asked. "Who's in charge here?" Grace asks in Kathleen's poem. is anyone in charge? what would I do about it, baby or no baby, finally I did not have to make that decision. made in the dark. the blood. garbage. it is all garbage, I told him. all this. reading the waste, the excrement. the entrails of animals. what's left in the cup. after the tea is gone, after the party's over.

—

Corrina may-caring in which all dance. getting to the bottom of it. here I had spent too much time in dreaming, acting the parts, a comedy of manners. a work, not to be sunk in it, but to be the spectator at that play. another one resists the distance. going about in the world, half-gasped, the spectacle. the little edges of horror wiped away. a mind sleeping.

it was a comedy of manners in which love is always trying to transcend wit. shut up. you talk too much. she was the one about whom her ex-husband said she never had an unspoken thought.

wonderful, the critique of wit. the critique of reason. a woman on the bus, demented, talking about another woman who had eight children. old mother Hubbard. getting the bone. saith Gertrude Stein: my little dog knows me. Lucky Pierre, Lynn's dog, knows her, is getting older, grayer with each passing year. this is wonderful. lying in bed I would never have thought these things.

the romantic love of ruins. *amor fati*. I myself have been a woman who longed to go crazy. loving my fate, embracing it. we would either be crazy or silent. I had gone both.

the critique of pure love. pure, what is it. submission. someone who will not take no for an answer. I think like a ouija board. lay your palm on the table. the answer must be yes or no. there are no other choices. do you follow? do you follow this line? the painted shadows running down the steps were blood. having something else dictate the decision. love or circumstance.

clocks.

—

Dear Rachel, about aphasia you're right, but she was she and really had it, unlike Mark who first suggested it years ago as an idea about poetry, how it is written anyway. of course it was right for me, stutterer, silent child. one day I would meet a real one, some other the wind blew through. she was tattered. a presence.

I would not have been a poet for all these reasons because I was indecisive. now I know. I could not drag it in. dragging it. the drowned mermaid. why, in her own element. it was not my element. neither air nor water. here they say one becomes acclimated. learning how to live in an artificial environment. it is called California but I'm not sure.

now we have to start from scratch but I have been on this trail for more than half of all the years I have lived. I have lost it for long stretches at a time. nevertheless. and I owe much to chance and circumstance, that which Derrida calls amor fati.

the reading of the writing goes on, this is for you because you are not here. you are always not here. you are never here. I make you up, I wonder how you look. and now it is so much easier to write than to speak. an other is so much an hallucination it's scary. I don't know what I speak to.

here, because you are not here, looking back I see it. myself in the swing in the backyard at the age of. six? alone. that will evoke someone's nostalgia. however you read it, each one thinks she is the only one. then we say it, as he said to me: "say it." to say. that this. writing. was not wholly lost. had not gone too far, far enough. by the life of me, down in the dirt.

that X which was laid over it ages ago. no wonder I am a woman. now. impossible. woman, that impossibility. that it takes place at all in any of us. "takes place." take it. there's a word for you. by god, it makes me angry to think that "take" appears here so easily, or any word, upon the 'mystic writing pad.'

all that flash in the pan, fly by night. it is heartless. I had no heart for it. it is what is lost that must be claimed. not found (impossibility) but claimed as loss. to say it.

—

San Francisco
March 5 – April 20, 1979

Dear Rachel, about aphasia you're right, but she was she and really
        Roman Jakobson
had it, unlike Mark who first suggested it years ago as an idea
    language,   forgotten   this theory, this disease as metaphor
about poetry, how it is written anyway. of course it was right
    stutterer
for me   child. one day I would meet a real one, some
    silent
                   contiguity disorder
other the wind blew through. she was tattered. a presence.

I would not have been a poet for all those reasons because I was
inconsolable
        . now I know. I could not drag it in. dragging it.
indecisive.
the drowned mermaid. why, in her own element. it was not my
element. neither air nor water. here they say one becomes
acclimated. learning how to live in an artificial environment.
it is called California but I'm not sure.

now we have to start from scratch but I have been on this trail

ribbon
string
thumb
birdbrain
a calling

compulsively overdetermined
circular or linear
switchback or spiral

for more than half of all the years I have lived. I have lost it
birdcrumbs marginalia
for long stretches at a time. nevertheless. and I owe much to chance and
circumstance, that which Derrida calls amor fati.

the reading of the writing goes on, this is for you because you are not here.
you are always not here. you are never here. I make you up, I wonder how
you look. and now it is so much easier to write than to speak. an other is so
much an hallucination it's scary. I don't know what I speak to.

here, because you are not here, looking back I see it. myself
"We suggest that naming, always originating in a place (the *chora*,
in the swing in the backyard at the age of. six? alone. that
space, 'topic' subject-predicate), is a *replacement* for what
will evoke someone's nostalgia. however you read it, each one thinks
the speaker perceives as an archaic mother –
she is the only one. then we say it, as he said to me: "say it."
a more or less victorious confrontation, never finished with her.
to say. that this. writing. was not wholly lost.
By indicating, as precisely as possible, how the units
had not gone too far, far enough. by the life of me,
and minimal operations of *any language* (and even more so those
down in the dirt.

that X which was laid over it ages ago. no wonder I am a woman.
of discourse) revive, model, transform, and extend the pregnancy
now. impossible. woman, that impossibility. that it takes place
that still constitutes the ultimate limit of meaning
at all in any of us. "takes place." take it. there's a word for
where, if analysis is lacking, transcendence takes root."

". . . the entry into syntax constitutes
you. by god, it makes me angry to think that "take" appears here
a first victory over the mother,
so easily, or any word, upon the 'mystic writing pad?'

all that flash in the pan, fly by night. it is heartless. I had
a still uncertain distancing of the mother, by the simple fact of naming . . ."
no heart for it. it is what is lost that must be claimed. not
(impossibility)
found but claimed as loss. to say it.

*Intertext from Julia Kristeva: "Place Names" in *Desire in Language*.

Broken:
San Francisco
May 9, 1983

Briarcombe
Bolinas, California
August 25, 1983

Six

Ron says what 'is brilliant but all wrong? *Phallus the first division, woman atomized,* what is that to him, to me, not that, but that also. that and not that, not being there, not there, an other waiting, *the* negative space, since all that is (real) defines it.

what is real in this fantasy of the real is the phallus. everybody believes it. I believe it. you can't touch it with a tenfoot pole because it isn't there. that's how it comes to be real. it isn't there. and I'm not here. nobody's here and that's reality. reality is we're all ghosts. dead souls, more than enough.

how come. this is a pretty pass. how did you get in that mess, scrape, scram. jiggers, the bulls. called the pigs, the nightmares on us eating us alive. my father skins the cows, I go from one to another trying to find my way. my teeth are still in my head, my eyes are dim I cannot see I have not brought my specs with me.

jazz. bad, o man, it was so bad. you should see it man, it was all the way live, hellabad, fucked up. meat out, hanging. cut up. at work on a body, the words are the most real things yet, you stop, it stops you when you realize it is a forbidden sexual act.

the way in is through the helicopter now shuddering by. looking for what is not there, empty. what's in it, snakes abound. never fixing on the thing itself, too gone, gone on you. one of these, I told him, and we have to share it. he said there was only one ring. I possess it. odd to think of that as possession. cling to it. the ghostly whereness. behind the veil. these tears. the downstream.

what not. the great shelf. little objects. her little thing. advancing towards it. the end. whatever the end will be. my love. you must take her ring but not by force only if she willingly offers it. he disarms us by playing the fool. but really he does the most horrendous, that does he do, in the name of the mother.

that's the way it is in all those stories, I told her. the harmless little brother, the last son. he is supposed to be witless. how much he really knows is anyone's business. here take care. sometimes it is wiser to question.

I had gone out of myself, double focus. an image and its ghost. the projector stuck, the film burning on the screen before our very eyes. before my very eyes he appeared and was witness. I raised my right hand. I swore to tell the truth. for that I was dismissed.

gizm, the smell of mushrooms, fungus in my cunt. there are no roads there. it is a territory still largely unknown, fabulous, what they looked for in the fog for years, the northwest passage, the great river from east to west, crossing the continent, the mouth of the Columbia. history has poisoned it, reclusive, still there, unregarded. the ghost of a journey. a memory of Orange county.

all this was a deliberate forgetting, the hollyhocks in summer, their little skirts we made dolls of, her memory of oleander so different from my own. *différant*. to differ and to defer. to put it off. waiting. advent. in which the whole world awaits a birth. the difference. one who is different. an other.

terror, the first word lighted, brushed across my eye, my eye, mother said, in that version. a chain of tears, one tear for every year, how summing up a year in that single painted drop.

there is no body one can own, nobody, it is gruesome, ignorant. there is no habitation. no home. I am not someone who resides here. no self within. the abuses of metaphor. knock at my door, we are all one here. fading out, we never saw her. this was a way to be.

I was following it. I had thrown a lot of junk in that hole where it sank out of sight. you knew it because the water backed up. this was a plumbing problem. in a very simple way. pipes and ashes. the cop was smoking his pipe while watching the mock fight.

for me it is all torture, teacher, mother. it is all about the stars. the secret cause. what rebellion. against it. she subverts it, I told him, by being unorganized. that is a structure. a structure is unconscious. we do not know why we are forbidden it. the love of a sister or mother. to go against it is death.

the penalties have been so severe for so long we wonder whether there is any way to undo the crime. to take it back. something provides the motive, an extreme in both directions. the outcome was a sense of self bearing it, however badly. I thought of my mother spending her youth at the sewing machine. and it goes back millions of stitches, a reign, the king sat in his counting house counting all his money.

hey nonny nonny. nonsense. we begin by blackbirds.

after the chain-link fence the chase. it can mean nothing other. the shadowy

figure beside him whose protection he will not secure. the dream of the
wolf man, the four-sided triangle, the dogs silent in a tree, an escape. it is
forbidden because it is always a mother, I can't fuck her, she belongs to me,
a memory I can't evade.

I know that I have all the time in the world, that I have refused the conditions so acceptable, that I have resisted, not knowing, that I would never
give myself to it, and thereby seem privileged. I was not. why does it seem
to be a question beyond choice? a will, what is it.

in the rain, falling with it. no way to force that. one is not duty bound.

fixed on it, I could not take it lightly, it assumed enormous proportions. it
was the narcissistic all in all, the gaze of the face in the mirror. the word was
empty because it was too full. full of my own meanings, that was the false-
ness. lying with memory. a movement forward towards death, in that I have
deceived you. you must not believe anything I do here. I do this in memory of you. it is an absence.

a power which is no power. a display of wounds. all that should have
remained hidden, obscene, a great need, a lack.

if sexual difference is disavowed he will desire to be the phallus for the
mother and become the lost object. if sexual difference is acknowledged he
possesses the phallus through identification with the father. he has it anyway.
there is only one of these, I told him, and we have to share it. and you have
the only ring, he said.

if sexual difference is disavowed she

if sexual difference is disavowed she
will be more complicated

a step in the right direction, a conspiracy of sons and lovers, against the
father. I am not talking about anything real. conceivably what is real is
rational, what is rational is real. this in relation to that, the unconscious

structure, the lacunae in the writing, the emperor's new clothes, only a fool would say that, in one innocent thrust gouging out his eye.

to think it, this ran along beside you, on the way, that double. the shadowy figure.

the equation: girl=phallus=baby.

the distance. not so buried. I know how far away it is, it is not there, never possible. distractions are to forget that. most work is to forget that.

'walking by the American River on Christmas Day.' there, the absence of my life, absent-minded.

here a necklace, the beads strung, the strands, here you may count it.

Dora had been Freud's subject, his content, she was not to be trusted. a wily mind. she knew what she wanted. she was playing with fire.

it is a completion of a fantasy. it is that.

he would say: 'you will know it before I do.' I did not want to know it. I was afraid of such knowledge. after such knowledge what life. the photograph of Artaud as a young man in *The Passion of Joan of Arc*. the photograph of Artaud as an old man, mad, gone, out of a life, why.

in films the streamers of life.

the banners, the flags. whatever is in the wind.

martyred women. in *Metropolis* she is not burned as herself but as a robot. it was the robot-woman who misled you, it was she who was passionate, greedy. she who was the witch. 'he was – he feared – such a castrated/castrating woman.'

wavering. staying on to see it to the end. on the line. the wherewithal, the wolf man. he looked at Freud and said yes. that was right. Wittgenstein thought there ought to be a rule. some authority. some one should be able to decide. one. where yes always meant yes or no, no. that is not the way it is done. the way it is done. write this. write this. write this. write this. write another word. this.

a white space intervening.

a white space intervening, white, white. that white light, static. questioning the first draft. this is not a literary work, I told him, this is not fussy. this is not my mother dusting the daisies. this is not domestic duty. this is not the idea. a preconception. this is it. the baby. the corpse. you can take that body and cut it up forever. this is a metaphor. a something. a meaning carried over. from one thing to the next. these are my leg hairs. the short hair that grows at the edge of my lips. lips, teeth. this is my little bow mouth. here it is. you will never know what I mean. when I say you I mean me. erasing all the *I*'s and using instead the third person. it alternates. an alternation, or alteration of generations. it changes. in other words. i.e., it changes. that is to say, it changes. it alters. it becomes something else, though its original form is still visible. one can trace that. he put a mark over it, a cross, but the word could still be read beneath it. 'the effacement of the trace?' to deface it, to cross it out, with a knife, to scar her face, his legs, that gesture, to whip the knife out, to scar it, the sign, these words do not match the thought. we will put an end to that longing. what thought there was we do not know. we will never discover it. it is not there. it is gone, or it never existed. impure. a fig leaf, someone said, of my imagination. covering it.

—

a recognition, entering the tomb, that was it, they had found it: *Ocian in view. O, the joy!* in sight, the lowlands.

—

burdened with those fantasies the real animal was lost. real, the animal itself, a form, of life, to be in its own place, studied, known, to be able to see it for what it is. undo this, on the track of it, it wavered in the sand. as recently as yesterday. we have corrupted nature and we have done it as children. the

—

perverse fantasies of innocent children. not. not. we were not.

we have done it ourselves as children. a mistake. carrying that original mistake all our lives with us into it. a reading. Freud's analysis of a phobia in a five-year-old boy: tell him it is all nonsense. it is. it is all nonsense. the horse, the dog, the snake. it is all nonsense.

—

setting off the air was gray. we were paying our own way. she said she wanted disjunction. it was there anyway, you didn't have to plan for it.

or in another version it happened another way. he bound her. hands behind her back. our criminal fantasies. you don't, she said, have to pinpoint it. we were traveling on another road. darkness fell. the lacunae in the case study. that version. 'upon that omission he fixed his gaze.'

backing and filling. was this a gardening term or did it come from auto mechanics. printing, writing. back and fill. painting, a war. to make a bloody hole. the policy of scorched earth. the turn of the screw.

'The derisive remark was once made against psychoanalysis,' says Ferenczi, 'that the unconscious sees a penis in every convex object and a vagina or anus in every concave one. I find that this sentence well characterizes the facts.'

back and fill. pottery.

in your absence I made these longing noises. it spreads. the voices. grading. the gorgeous kimono. the other side of this is another term, conservative. right on the edge. plucking the guitar, music fills the whole house. house cries. lay me down. air.

'To say that O began to await her lover the minute he left is a vast understatement: she was henceforth nothing but vigil and night.'

nothing but vigil, night adore, stormy day or softly. awaiting her lover she was nothing. nothing but night. nothing. nothing doing.

Cinqo de Mayo. save the day, god save her, the queen. frog's in the well, distracted. I didn't know what time it was. I thought of someone's servant. I thought o will I fall in love with her. her sexy feet in torn black stockings.

she, she who was another pronoun. she. awaiting her lover. the feeling which arrests the mind. the other side of this. getting to the bottom of it, I said. o lord, I desired to desire thee. a master. some other to whom. nevertheless not my will.

frothy, early. early one morning just as the sun was rising.

o don't deceive me o never leave me. a synthesis.

—

'back and fill: 1. To manage sails so that they alternately catch the wind and lie idle, thereby keeping the boat in a river channel and floating with the current. 2. To take opposite positions alternately.'

the alternation of generations. the hypocritical remark spoken out of both sides of the mouth at once. butter wouldn't melt.

a father in love. did you think you were someone else? beyond the pleasure principle the language poets, an introduction.

—

cloudy, here I think of the several stains, layers, cheese, wallflowers, the tomatoes. these metaphors drawn from nature, domestic activity. beyond the message. o mama.

in a cloud, a fiend hid in a cloud.

all that was hidden shall be revealed. on that day. on the day of reconcilia-
tion. those mysteries. *you're* a poet, he said.

marginalia. this life. I said the insubstantiality, that they were ghosts,
phantoms, that's what she did, she preserved that.

the unearthliness, their footprints in the sand. where have we been. what
have we here. waking in the morning with clear and certain knowledge. I
am too old to be taken lightly, too ancient, Diana of the crossroads, Hecate.
furrowed. my brow. some witch in her also. she admitted it. if so, what so, if
that is a power name it. women have died for it, it is not to be taken lightly.

that is not you, he said, and I said you are afraid of it. we eat, we drink, we
sleep, we screw.

here we are, an old story, another old story. backing off. that is not you. yes.
it was an outward display of the symptoms, the wounds. I was cut. you cut
me. the wound healing beneath your hand. you did not know that. I am
telling you now.

seeing it through in this 'non-repeating universe', the repetition compulsion.
each word falls where it may, non-repeatable. here is a world, shall I speak
it. in the 'background, that vow.' to our animal lives, as he might have said.
what is it we take from animals, all that was holy originally. to ask it is to ask
what is a body.

the world is a vow. steady. mind a great matter, the matter of Troy, I said,
after all these years, still after all these years. I am not used to it. it is new.

lay these words down so they will be less cloud-like, my head is not the sky.
the beat, the rhyme. this rhymes with that, he said, turning the pages. for
the sake of auld lang syne. the old long sigh. the birth of the family.

in the myth of the unicorn the Lady collaborates. she, lovely, is working for
the enemy, a spy, a trap, a snare. a man's lady. she comes on the scene. of
course the unicorn is innocent, the child's body, slain. for her sake. lovely

lady. our mother. lay your head in my lap. the seductive virgin. no wonder she is sentimentalized, her rolling eyes, as she bears the son. the dead son.

her part. that is not you, he said. but it was. it was some part of me disowned, disavowed. to reclaim it is to see that she was not first one and then another but the same. she is involved in it, implicated, silent, it is her silence we cannot bear, she is lovely.

he paws the ground, snuffles before her, what does he think she is? how does he know she is beautiful. strange, illiterate beast. who taught him beauty?

and what does she think. what does she think she is doing there, sitting under the trees, her blonde hair, her downflowing milky, her eyes, what does she see. when he is captive at last does she look away in horror, "O god, I cannot save my child from death." how does she fare, pretty lady, in this world, captive, a maiden in both camps, nothing but beauty, illusory.

a reclamation of the 'occult and impure? jagged.

a jagged hill of corn, a row of green beans, some turnips, throw that in the stew. in the desert. pentecostal.

foreign, her foreign eyes. one would be exiled, I would sing you one-o. the river of the lady. the sound the trees make when she is spring, the sound of insect hum. we both loved her, swore allegiance to her. I a child and you a man. 'I a child and you a lamb.' we have been innocent after great difficulty, after wars among powers, fought out early and secretly. then we begin our lives. as innocent children. all it masks, little lamb who made thee. and Blake, who saw so many things upside-down and so shook the truth out, partly, still had the songs of innocence precede experience.

our little little. our little thing. our little secret. our slash. our wound. our drawn up and wrinkled. our dirty mouth. child's play. it is all in the mind. we lost it at an early age. so long ago we don't remember. "let me remember, let me forget": Helen to Theseus, H.D. to Freud. let me be done with it. let me go. let me know so that I can be done with it. that is not you, he said. not now. little child, who made thee? our father, the lamb. o lamb of god, I come. in which the universe is redeemed of the perverse fantasies of children.

—

San Francisco
April 21 – May 12, 1979

Seven

here no well, true, hear no, what, that true enough, that dear but not enough, naught, a tie, leaning, out on it, my i.d., yes, where U WANTED to be, our only, make a break into that open territory, fast away. too much myself to be you. too much his fingers, gone, an absence. too much his lovely only ass. the mole in the corner of his back, my hand always, too far away to think it was anyone else but me, but you are here, a blue-eyed shine, nothing tough, rosy delivered, a boo-boo, a mouth boy, or hand that I held, another that I shouldn't lean, far and away, his whole, that I try to clear, not a chance, his leaning over the plant, the fire, I would be me, watching, I, I would say come here, I would say the small of your back, my hand there, you, that not in me, another definition, a solo. how in love with myself I'm a woman's body.

but some man that you were, a flock of hair, a turning, when you turned to me, some length not wasted, and maybe fragile, some just marvelous orchid, you were,

something to grow, ever, that soft with what your arms you, if I said it, body, the brow, head absolutely, your finding out me, your one, that you are, continues, moving, swells, high, up in me, home.

—

a hand-sewn garment, a flag.
a drippy posture
nothing wasted nothing gained. testing.

what we just went through will anybody tell me. clouds airbrushed.
the sight of something anterior. where it all happened before.
before that and before that.

the garden in the dark. do you want to go to a garden party? I asked. plains
comma the great. the great outback.

orchid, his in stained glass, I had no recollection of the film in which the
last scene is a stained glass tulip. and then recalled it perfectly. on the day
after yesterday. the today show, if we deepen the knowledge we increase the
ambivalence and stop. Hamlet, the double bind.

from the bottom up. leaping. so much more in than out. a dream. but
then, I said, I begin to feel like a ghost, one of those wandering spirits,
unquiet, not decently buried, a soul on the moor, my rags around me,
nothing finished, no rest, nothing finished.

finished
never done

'Writing is that forgetting of the self, that exteriorization, the contrary of the
interiorizing memory. . . It is this that the *Phaedrus* said: writing is at once
mnemotechnique and the power of forgetting.' Derrida.

remember by forgetting. that grace of attention. that attentiveness to the
materials, that argument, he said, with the material, and that would be that
place where it was not all smoothed out, over. that would be its meaning.

over and out over and out. the crackling of voices, the wisp of dogs,
barking. never done. an opening into it. a round forest magnified. we came
there. I forgot it immediately. I said I want to drop this, I want to lay this
down, not carry it, are you still carrying that stone? I wanted to be done

with it. done in that lightly. done in that I could carry something, anything, a physical memory, a bank, a computer. store of it. in it, all there, not wandering in the dark among those circuits, the *I Ching* reminds us constantly no blame. no blame is nothing settles. no fat in the arteries. the heart. the heart is clean, 'it strengthens the heart.'

forever a book that we loved, these were models of stories, likely to be repeated since the number of plots is only about seven. but we aren't interested in plots anymore, traps, let the light shine, through those holes, the negative space, the darkness through it. I said: it was the best demonstration of negative space I ever saw, it made waves of darkness. the light was diminished. created the darkness as if light were the ground and not the other way, you would have it, so he said let there be dark. it is all light anyway.

we know we live in an expanding universe because of the night sky. if we did not have a dark sky at night then nothing. nothing as we know it. then generation. in the wake of an original catastrophe. the catastrophe which began it.

forever a book that we loved. inside and outside. back and forth in the light, in the shadow. waving. waves of light. a wave, peristalis. the opening of the intestine, the opening of the field. like a fiend hid in a cloud. fellow, follow a bonny cow low. that lowland smell. the words write. *écriture*. crossing boundaries, these signs from another tongue. on the frontier the agricultural station censors incoming bugs. imagine a universe where the sun could be regarded as right or wrong.

recent sections from a reading. in which. peripheral vision, she said. pick pick. the grass bloomed. I was not talking about anything unusual. she said that writing was more like nature, that you had to make sense of it the way you'd make sense of a natural object.

bitter lemons on that tree which no one harvests. the full moon. abundance is all. more than we need, more than you know. a surplus economy.

a build-up of words. would the religious impulse disappear in a wholly rational economy. what is real is rational: the future of an illusion. Moses in the bullrushes, another baby got the blues. the blues, a downer, wasted on reds. the wasted shape, the critical mass. the garden steamed. the invention of the steam engine changed the world. an iron horse pounding inexorably across the flatlands, the grasses of Nebraska, of India. one ear to the ground we listened for its coming. it beat and shook. o my mother. she sat and listened for the nightbirds, for the moon, for the train hooting. lonely as an owl. pinching feathers. she said her mother warned her against those people because they do terrible things with chickens. she spun the hen over her head. dead it lay on the carpet. looming.

I have called it into question I question it. the question why is a quest. in these days I was given to the sun, to morning work, to plants and animals. yellow-eyed grass. violas. cucumbers, chrysanthemums.

what is apparently there, a long-legged begonia and a flat circlet of new leaves at its feet. that for love, a permanent absence. a shared sleep. in Beulah the beautiful vegetable kingdom.

therefore water and weed. the cat scrapes by me. my skin taking on the impression of the sun. those shadow prints of ferns, of leaves. I buried my head in her. the maidenhair.

blue-eyed daisies, yellow-eyed grass. it will like to get out of its pot. it will like to walk around the garden. pity, it will pity you, it is a mercy that beauty. death is a mercy and so also is beauty.

my father's a tree, he dropped his branches. that could be a tree, that could be parsley and lettuce.

this interminable work is women's work, it is never done, it is there again and again. I live here, an unreconstructed housewife.

the vines, the grape ivy clinging. it will save you. soften the lines. the grape-stakes, the fence posts going by by by on the road, a shadow, the shadow of the vertical on the yellow-eyed grass in the early afternoon. it would take full sun, it would be happy there. little person. this is all pathetic fallacy. this world is not my home.

—

an unnamed wish, a countertransference. that she took no responsibility for her desires, her

whatever must be done we are not the victims purely. a hard pill to swallow. the male bias of psychoanalysis, the male bias of everything. the masculine protest.

as pale as the moon the sky barked. whistling girls and cackling hens always come to no good ends. noon.

no one, a man with a moon face in an arm chair, arrrum, filigree. decorating the words. he said they wouldn't accept him as a patient at the Psycho-analytic Institute because he had been tampered with. his neurosis wasn't in a pure state.

whatever surely she must be very far away. how did he do it at that moment in history, floundering. a leopard shark.

a fallen skin, sinking faster than

keeping up with it, to arrive at the same time. to do one and the other at once, being her I was also him. myself as the cowboy. a polarized marriage. she will be she and he he. but ivy is sacred to the god Dionysus and grows in dark places.

whatever in the world behind closed eyes the doors whispered. let her be. let her be her. let us be as if we were not forever entwined in that, as if we were not able to unthread the conclusions, deliver ourselves of the plot. at that level she intercedes for you. she cries mercy at the feet of the father. she knows where he is at the far corners of the universe. he has removed himself. he has gone off to sit and brood beyond the pale of light. if not that then this. but we had opened it. the knife that cuts both ways. always. in the center of it the rose. pure. the flaming heart, an artifact. believe me. this is not a special dispensation. this is a matter of life and death.

falling faster than the thing ahead of you. 'You have to dive down, as it were, and sink more rapidly than that which sinks in advance of you.': Kafka.

they were gone, fleeting. her lips, eyes. a romance, a cue. I heard her say something to you. to what does this refer? shall I go on worrying about Dora? a famous misunderstood lady.

out of body, out of sight out of mind. the baby knows. if it isn't there it isn't there. everything else is hallucination.

words are halfway houses to lost objects. we are sick in them. despair in them. lost, mirrored in them. lost in a hall of mirrors. infinite regression. he kept shooting her image until she lay dead in a heap of broken glass.

broken, broken. she, what to do. who else I could be. a lady of no importance. she enters history paralyzed by desire. a mouth. a burning cheek. checked. lay that cross over it.

a mirror. an edge.

a gilded flame, the light picking the objects out one by one.

that dream is standing ankle deep in water. he flickered his toes. sirens calling the danger. those of us who had given up marriage forever. holy matrimony, on that score. the bonding of masters and slaves, established by custom, given sanction. only god can make a tree.

where o where my little dog.

get down. she said: just put on some of that low-down, jigaboo, fucking music and watch my mother dance. watching my mother dance.

wait.

orange and then orange and blue. falling faster than the thing ahead of you but nevertheless keeping behind it. 'In your own day you will be believed.'

from this life I was determined to look back. alienated.

settling out, I did not want to know particularly where it was. the truth floating to the top. whatever, it floats. it has all that air whipped in. the breath knocked out. not breathless, strangled, or shallow breathing, but the words for breath knocked out. a hit. a violent story. the children of paradise.

on the left side roses grow. the man in the truck on the bridge was wearing a gold band, a wedding ring on his left hand. odd to think he was married when he seemed such a vagabond. *homeboys* the girls write, and then we find our way through this. zero the fool.

———

that child, that little girl, what she trimmed, the various diseases boiled away, condensed, growing into some kind of order, now, I said to her 'that's how they should look.' speaking of the roses. to look in that thicket and see a plan. it will take more light. a southern exposure, 'east is a direction but not from here.' and he comes in, dark, submitting to it. a narrative bent, the events that led to its being there. one by one.

not to go against the grain. laid out, all the hair combed in one direction. the way the wind blows. the bending, in open places, in the plains, the low bending of the wheat, given to the wind.

given to it, wind and water, happening on the far side, never thinking of it. the little interiors, the refuges, a house in the woods, it was like myself. taking shelter in there we thought of ourselves as endless dark spaces inside. in all that one wanted to come home. some definition. a pot of violets in full sun.

think of it, a mirror, a reflective surface, where would you want it. what does it mean, a mirror. where to be so as to make sense. since that would be following it down to the third scion. a word whose usage in horticulture actually precedes, is the figure of, 'hence, a descendent,' along a line, certain parents, a tree, genealogical. tracing the stems and branches.

that freeing of the bond in nature. proliferation.

nothing we do can help it. let it have its own way. letting you have your own way, a rock garden. the skinned desert plants. my ferns. my home in the northwest. those soupy details.

going all the way how calm I looked they said. satisfied. something to be said for it. the interiorization of memory. the creeper. a vine he called a weed. what we value what we trust. it is not beautiful it proliferates.

comes floating out from behind the clouds but I knew that would happen anyway because the air was so warm. moist. the jungle plants, the palm, reading it. we had consulted the various oracles, there was a future we shared. out of certain complexities we drift and mesh or rub one another raw. it was not my time. fig leaves. summer, how it loves to grow in the summer, he said. a little season, Kathleen's summer poems.

they are the same as we are, lady ferns, lady palms, hooded, cobra, pitcher plant, 'a novelty,' augh, our simian cousins. the writhingness of everything, the snaky shoots of the morning glory twisting on the fence. everything spinning, that movement in waves.

there the am, the conditions of life. to be, at intervals, it comes. speaking of it to her. I thought wordless wonder. nothing to write home about. hunger and thirst after me. spiritual decline. one finds oneself not hungry. no accounting for appetites, for tastes. he said I was a sensualist, I didn't disagree. always.

there is a further side of the moon, a side we never see. there is a dark side, the 'unconsciousness of the unconscious' out of which some storms, indirection, a wind, a lunar wind from a long way off. there is no wind on the moon. is it a rock, is that the foundation, a mire, a swamp, a sandy place, wherever the house.

our something mother. our trip to Africa.

—

closed flies. open Sunday. who was Mr. Bones? writing it down then as now.
if you read this please don't laugh. therefore I bent over backwards. a display
of suffering, of the wounds.

she walked into the library in Atlantic City and swallowed arsenic. seven
years ago today. a sentence. these words: she walked into the public library
after work, on her way home from the office, sat at a table, and swallowed
arsenic. testimony.

damn it. a thimbleful of mercury. damn it. a hundred somethings. anything.
head in the oven. the lethal. not to believe you are you, not to be sewn up,
not to be aware of the mask, walking forward while pointing to the mask,
don't you believe it? making your mask and pointing to it, this is the form.
a possible form. of life.

a white light on the angel wing. that comfort, the consolation of the world,
of these gardens.

beginning anew. that we come to it.

a friend and a lover. his vines love to grow in the summertime, he said.
nubbly, nuzzling it, very, the damp ground. the air surrounding it. growing
up, space was not death. it paled out. someone I had gone beyond with.
that sad face of my little brother. holding him it will turn out another way.

our violet selves. do ye this in memory of me, in that this separation ends,
be with me this day in paradise. o De gone ahead of me, a trace now, fading, that you were there at all, turning, not to know, what a darkness sur-
vives, if you had survived.

—

that you could trace the line looking into that thicket, this writing, the light and the shade, editing the rosebushes accordingly, true to something, out there in the world. that would be. rambling, thorns.

what else is there? what else but that tap, bucket, our kneeling at the water. and so. from that day to this. preserving it. that world which is fragile, how.

a moon, the Rockies, the mountains in which you were. crestfallen. I came out on a high place looking back. there was where I had come from. here among stars, Olduvai, the canyon, the oldest bones. I was thinking of that line, of that longest line. a river and its tributaries. it doesn't look like that, this is a map.

in a budding grove, in a cocked hat, in a pig's eye. sermon. quoting chapter and verse. verso. folio. words for it. remembering. he would begin at A and read through the entire work. therein. finding out. stuffing our heads with it. her metaphor. some dumpy place, end of the line, staying slightly drunk on beer all the time, making a film.

wherever, people wandering, we talked about adventures, walking to New Orleans, a down and out waterfront bar. did you ever seriously think of spending much time in Chicago?

blank wall, skull on the laundry basket on top of some newspapers, just like a poet. it wasn't an argument about aesthetics I tried to tell her but she wanted to make it one. inside and outside. shut up. shut up, I wanted to say. *shut up you mout*. gramma waddling, my mother, you always were on the plump side, my other grandmother saying. ruffling her feathers. mama. ruffed grouse. she turns, then, her back to her. looks out the kitchen window. mother-in-law. to daughter-in-law. women in the same family. by marriage. friends and neighbors. kith and kin.

'Happiness is the deferred fulfillment of a prehistoric wish. That is why wealth brings so little happiness; money is not an infantile wish.'

consider the lillies. consider blue, clothed in it. consider my breasts, tanned and white below and tipped.

a run for your money, what child is this, what work you do. a drop in the bucket. to feel like an adult is to shoulder the guilt, to make a pack of it and carry it around. to be burdened. busy. to have no time, to be harrassed. doing a million things at once, divided. divided attention, to see beauty as a great question, not to see it but to ask instead whether it is there at all and why. doubting. there may be a center, god knows this is one, no one else will have seen it that way, will question it.

beauty is a mercy I said to her, there is no accounting for it. and death is its mother, but I wasn't thinking of that, I had to remind myself constantly of that these days, summer here, and yet. a twinge of fall yesterday. a twinge of that yellow smoky light. it is already accumulating. the days which issue.

—

looking around a world between sleep and waking. the gray violet tinged early morning, mornings come early, the coastal fog, the sense of fog drifting through this, knocked over the drink I wasn't holding falling asleep. dreaming already.

a grayed magenta. gray-eyed. his eyes, blank pain, a simple man.

one makes a gesture toward revelation. a gesture, a pause. a pen, a fancy quill, an article, a letter A, the handle to which all this is attached. I'm a little teapot.

a particular kind of sultry romantic drama associated with the '40's: movies set in tropical or semi-tropical places. she herself is the storm, the heat, the rain.

a potted palm.

a woman in the midst of an adventure, the scene by the lake, the top of the stairs, her slap on his cheek burning on her own. she coughed. it was her father.

a son, they might have preferred a son. a gate in the alley. walking there we went down to the garden. opened the gate, there it was. pool, stone mushrooms, little bridges, trains, the waterfall, the swing under the awning. a peculiar kind of mossy grass, never, imitating art, somewhere we have seen that. I said to her that beauty is a mercy. I said I don't want to argue about it.

'most thinking is censored dreaming,' most dreaming is censored thought. you might just as well say I eat when I sleep is the same as I sleep when I eat, it is the same thing for you. sleepy rodent, teeth and eyes, and she is a sly fox.

the sly brown fox or something jumped over the fat lazy dog. a dog's life, dogstar, dog days. the rank, the runt of the summer. of the litter. where they fell, the order, I said the cat was getting senile. I thought the word might have been senile but that made no sense in context. I had to invent something to make the meaning clear. something else. something else came to take its place. he said that you could tell by Bogart's smile that he was really enjoying the scene. and she had said he wasn't acting, he was really breaking up. breaking up, her little bench, like break-up furniture in the movies, I said. thoroughly broken. all at once it collapsed. waiting for the end. the thunder. it made him think of the holocaust. a lesson from childhood.

the lake country, the odds.

she doesn't let much get by her. she keeps an eagle eye out for it. thank god. that sort of woman. a woman of many parts. a man for all seasons. what the hell, he said, plant them in January. to have all one's faculties intact. dreaming secondhand. I was listening to her announce the time at ten second intervals. honey. shut up, sugar. shut up, kitty. a recorded voice. the record of an order. those roses now dead.

there fiddling around with orders again, there this and moving something else there the space shaping, playing with it, forgetting the serious person. the way he would have done it. I said something changes inside of me. in the kernel. the germ. the nut of it. it bore that impression. like seed. the relations of the tree to the nut. tree crops. a permanent agriculture. is it like anything.

'running around enough it may be perfect' maybe. fixing it up. imagining the eye moving in another direction. thinking of the mirror in an odd place, what might unexpectedly be reflected. to one's surprise and delight. he himself so fragile, bearing the idea of perfection.

there was something I saw, bore in mind, as I began shifting the pieces. what would satisfy the eye, that horizon. a line moving. at the very end a clump of trees. clumping along. fading into a mist. word clumps. clusters. they hover together. things things. the thinginess of it. spatial relations. time so beyond, living closer to the ground, a seed life.

seed clusters, harmonies. what satisfies the eye, shifting bodies. how I said something changes inside me. trying to think of it, what. not escaping. blue and white, dotted swiss. the names of fabrics, a woman's vocabulary. a different usage. using it.

a mother who buttonholed, I brought Jeremy a flower for his buttonhole but he wasn't wearing any, put it in my own, moss, running around enough, the cerebral cortex. it may be perfect, the kernel, the shell. broken into. diffuse cerebritis. an infection all over the surface. a bug, an invasion. something from the outside inside. there is something which is pleasure which is not experienced as pleasure. it is Pleasure. here we are where words are not common. Pleasure is not a common name, it is a ground, a territory, a proper noun, the name of a place. just as I. a place, 'where you are there arises a place? those names moving on boxcars, Great Northern, Southern Pacific, the Soo Line, Cotton Belt. moving lines, whatever was there, these will turn, changing in the Book of Changes, to something which is in opposition.

—

slid into first base just ahead of what was falling. what was falling both ahead and behind? what position to take up in relation to It? coming back they would make this analysis interminable, finding another set of words beneath the account already rendered by Freud. yielding another story entirely. another origin, another denouement. and yet he lived on, past all of them, as the Wolf Man, a famous literary character.

our lives other wise. other wisdom, clarity. the silence of the body, the actual organic core. that is not language, it is all hallucination.

—

and to do it sometime before Christmas, I said, when the weather will be too cold to drink gin and tonic.

cold, some weather I'm thinking of, the ivy around the pole. the pole star. an aptitude for it, a calling. a sign of the times. this rhymes with that, he said.

going to Chicago. I would rather the music had been jazz. I would rather the photography had not been so romantic. the theme and the subject. what appears here is a trace. tracing it, she traced the characters with her fingers. teaching them Chinese. a dream entitled: I am becoming a Chinese girl. la Chinoise. the failure. I am what I am.

a star, another way to go. I noticed the fish and the turtles in the aquarium kept arranging and rearranging themselves into patterned groups. what pleases the eye. an aesthetic experience, a perfect wineglass. perfecto. to think, she said, they do it all with sand. who would have thought it? to turn sand into that? the transformations.

the romanticism of the western landscape, some sign of wilderness left. blue delft. blue and white and some strong black lines. then. o darling, our love. she is their darling, let me call you sweetheart. winning the battle, losing the war. a us. a successful operation but the patient died. having given his consent. one of a thousand and he had to be that one.

four centuries of women poets. lives of writing. waiting. she who waits also serves. it is true that Sex is masculine, nothing would get done without it. forging ahead, the active principle. what, I thought, am I that he uses me so?

on the third day I embarked for the promised land. these are narrative sentences and not statements. they are suspended. fictions. holding the breath, breathlessly, to watch it, how it will progress, what will be the outcome, the end. in the entrails a knot. with all those miles and miles. but he answered

—

and said they stay pretty much the way they were laid out. and who did that? these are questions, seeking the secret cause. this is not phenomeno-logical. this believes there is a secret cause.

the Ace is like a big heart blooming out there. and I could wish all my days to be bound each to each. by natural piety. whatever that is, she wrote these things are of nature. trees, rocks, flowers, a desert. have a desert, have an ocean. think of living down there, there would be other fish swimming around, strange plants growing. that too would be nature, let's not be too hasty to define it. there's a thin moving line. blurred edges. if it were there as sharply as Blake wanted who would get over the boundary in the middle of the night. they were living close to the border in northern Italy, 'we need some new genes' he said. he remembered the *nor* and thought I was Norwe-gian, someone from the north originally. someone, a Svenska-Suomalainen.

all that was a foreign language, something she was learning, Navajo. o my horse. the corn in the east. somewhere over the rainbow. blue skies. it's shaping up and I wasn't even thinking about it. it grows. hard and soft, she wrote. hard buds, nipples of buds. hardening. I take you. his

oleander. his skinny, the slight boy's brown body.

'the brown boy's slight body.'

the copper light falling on the brown boy's slight body is carnal fate, the fate, the destiny of meat and beans. how we are all in that, so unseen. the fate of sand, to become glass.

mother pie. pooky pooh. babbling. as if language were not his native speech, or speech were not his native tongue. some people so unhappy talking. writing because you have writer's block, a cramp in the leg.

be thou.

being and time. in time we see. seeing it that way for the first time. o lovely I said his lovely eyes beginning the day babbling to make sense of it in the other other in the green world or some darker name to only whatever if you. and that union holding an image of hierarchy but there are, there are hierarchies in nature, are there? the base and the superstructure. what changes. something deeply settled between us, but that wasn't true, not then, and not now. a wish devoutly to be. consummated. *consummatum est.* the sum of it. the whole and its parts. partial, that was a partial solution, solving it day by day, and then I saw it. the whole cycle from fern to spore to fern. o yes. there it is in time. just in time. floating. it unhooks disjoints comes floating to the top. why an invasion, of privacy, privacy comes floating to the top, some dirty some non-dying thing, that obscenity, not to die, that dirty wish for immortality, sludging it, sledge, hammer or sled, dragging it, over snow.

the immortality ode. breakfast. dropping manna.

your teeth, a tongue. gondola. teeth, a tongue, a dark. putting his finger in her mouth. in her mouth. the weird way in which the world gets in the way. rattle, rattle. getting into it. filthy marriage. opal. a silver drawn out dark, the new moon. a halo. finding food, water, there in the desert. she said that too, that desert was a nature.

shut up, kitty. I can barely remember her, I said, she's been dead for so long now. never never land. poets with their heads in cloud and cuckoo land. the world split open.

George Oppen. broken. then I stepped into the shower last night or the night before. the beads broke. a sure sign. a sacrificial victim. totalled out. the sum of it. she said they got softened up for the kill. I thought how awful, none of us can afford it. scraping the paint off the windows. a memory of the future, he saw himself sitting in a hotel room maybe, was it, twenty years from now? and what was there. the end of it. locked out.

looking for the buds hard as nipples, rising, a view of the rising sun, the new moon rising or setting, the sky falling, the sky and its movements that's all we have left she said I was cold walking and then the sun came out we were walking along at night. the clock, the virgin wisps, my angel hair, its color, fern, I want her close to me, that female, the womanly thing, their roundness in the bath, my own angularity. honey. let me call you sweetheart. fed up. that's how I am.

I was holding on with both hands. listen up. 'If the base determined the superstructure, then art would progress along with everything else . . .' Greek art flourishing only in Greek society. but it doesn't there is something out of time.

little noises, honey love. laving. over the district. love lies deeper than anger. the only only. deeper than anger nothing says no.

real suffering is not her her fault. she has no magic. there is no way to cure it. let go.

a dream of passion, a year in the hinterlands. o little budding leafy all bright stars. little sonorous, a small song, a deep voice.

furry rubbers. noisy dogs. I've been your dog since nineteen sixty-four. when I was young.

a confusion of errors, non sequiturs, I wasn't thinking of it. it was that. precisely what is unthought, it retreats. Hiding. the coast of Oregon confined in mists. we go out. finding fairyland, dreamland. a sky yielding to it. that's what I wanted. that's what I always wanted. that attention, that act of union, of holding together. the young fool.

robed for Pentecost, the day of the descent of the holy spirit. rough winds do shake the darling buds of May. around. something, the pole in the center, commemorating that shaft, field of pain or pleasure. in this sign. I have come to the end. I am already approaching it. contemporary, he said. in this time. catching up with it I was running, he was running to school, that boy, oneself as a child, wherever they are, breaking the ice, stooping to it, she stoops to conquer, saving the day. she who also rides out with the candles, pentecost, that blithering spirit which fell on her with a vengeance, and a father purifying himself, this fathers' world. This is My Father's World. trespassers will.

renegade charms, eyes in the dark. god knows what they turn into in the dark, charmed animals, under a spell, they grunt and smell. sniffing around, it must be an illness, we grow up to it, we have a taste for it, developing a taste for beer, tobacco, a taste for death. not to make much of it.

non fluencies. in the crypt there is a false Unconscious. proud. a will which runs that deeply to protect the father. his name. if that is so. so and so. if beneath it all the will to protect the father runs so deeply. not that the truth will out. but a perfect fabrication, producing dreams, associations. what is there. what flowering clematis, woman tree, rubber plant. along the fault. if it fell apart along these lines there was another story. in which the son was a liar in order to protect the father.

whatever comes, here and then gone, *fort/da,* the mother's face of peeka-boo. here and then gone, a peekaboo universe, 'the baby knows that objects don't exist when they are out of sight.' out of sight out of mind. out of it. a prevailing mind, a wind, a 'scandal of sound.' whatever covers it. Japanese folding screens, lacquer, or pure distilled alcohol flavored with juniper ber-ries. keep my skillet good and greasy all the time.

in the breaks another name, another message to read. poking around with this stick, poking, words stick, poem, poema, what if Mary were a virgin. what if it were true I won't get what I want, shouldering it. a burden, I said, what you can carry. he was thinking of wild horses. running with it. in the break, breach, nothing would be healed. breech. the break and its cover.

covering it, the alibi for the father. why the father is law, the stone. if the alibi for the father runs so deeply, if that is the lie on which. the fundamen-tal silence, that there is a third, and he is the father, intervening. the inter-vention of the father. and yet the deepest unnameable is that vow to the mother: I will not abandon you. that secret, fought out on all fronts, I will not abandon you. a mother, herself. the prehistoric judgment.

—

these are the facts of our lives, there are accidents, there is blind fate. faith. there is the brick that falls out of the sky. not as individuals but as a species they were successful. arachnids. who were we as a species that was lost. the successful slaving away. submerged in a pattern you would not see the end of. looked front and back and could not see the end of that line. moving in the street. mass. mass. weight volume. mass, holy. mass comma holy. originally what is holy is what we take from the beasts. we know our lives are holy in the mass, in that union, keeping still, holding together. a wind, a natural force, a flood, something given. that that's not it. there is nothing given in human nature. nothing that cannot be changed. I wonder how far I will go with that. I wonder if I think there is some rock on which, even then, there is not, this universe is not eternal, it began, there's no rock that solid.

a spear, a blandishment. loading zone. in the zone, a three-way split. unicorn. a blue cut glass lamp from West Virginia. these stories, heart-shaped, staying the night in Noe Valley, that was another country. all that. clear sighted. making things asymmertical, off-center. just slightly off. I was interested in the shapes. the overlap. this is a story about myself, I told her, how stubborn I am. how rigid. how I told her and she understood my anger at those side wings, every bit as phony and just a piece of decoration as a tacked on carved rose. it serves, however, to prove, to provide.

—

in this heat a bird. blue, blue and white, a dinner party. women, they did it, they went always mad. it was a way to go. there us. there is a bell, the cathedral bell.

moiré.

shifter, shape-changer, changing phonetically usually according to Grimm's law. the secret cause. the secret cause is grave and constant, is it, there is no image for it, molecules, or atoms, or whatever the tiniest thing can split, one becomes two, and so on to infinity. the end of time. to end it. it is a consummation devoutly to be wished. a struggle. falling or failing at the fault lines. holding together, the secret shares, sharer, the double, you, her face in the cracked mirror, a swan's neck bared. the mirror illusion, the sign of female vanity.

seeing herself a child, the sun shining more brightly now having come out from behind a cloud, but it was the cloud that moved suddenly, blown, scuttled.

don't do it to her, let her be. propping up those illusions. but she would not have said that. she would not have said up the waterspout. if she were a woman and not a surrogate male.

roses, we toll, tell. ringing the bell, already dead at the beginning of the play, the secret cause, the fathers squandering.

from beginning to end. an end foreshadowed, the shapes of events falling in front of us, trying to fall faster, to keep us, to be there, to meet you when you come home. don't wait for me. I told her. but she was already dead. dead at the beginning of the poem, the play. Blanche the white woods in spring, she said, but I always thought of snow, of the winter. of dead wood bleached white, of the desert, or wood beached. covering a scandal of sound. these things at the limit of reason. these dreams undone. that was where he lived his life, in city fields. gas pipes and subdivisions. dividing the vision.

she said she saw how the telling of the story, the alibi, self-justifying. it is fortunate to. the *I Ching*. literature itself is interminable. but somehow the analysis must come to an end. a terminal as a point of embarcation also. going away. north to Oregon. as far as I can see.

what is homelike becomes unhomelike. we scattered, the Jews, now everybody wanders. unfortunately. we have taken that burden. it is a pack on his back.

a fate not. not crowned. not sought, nevertheless my moth pursed. mouth, moth, fluttering, the folded wings of my mouth. faded. not teleological I said to him. not as if it had a purpose, not a goal, not somewhere to go, no terminal. lighten up, you guys. who said that. someone yesterday must have said that but I can't remember.

if you play hide and seek this way, *fort/da,* letting the left hand, if this then that.

a checkerboard. she was the Red Queen. Regina.

word. again. word. there was another territory but this already determined the windings. Kai Winding. that backwater, or slough, a rowboat with daddy. into that. if a watery grave, she came there, there is a willow grows aslant a brook. Ophelia's fate, the daughters. joining hands. a circle dance, a circuit. the farmer in the dell. slats.

fiery tongues. lingua, that thing that flickers in the backyard. in the garden, in my father's house there are many mansions. she was struck by that passage, thinking it very beautiful, struck by it, the. mirrored in silver, verbal a non-separation. why the flowers? why sometime color, flowers doing it, coloring themselves, in response to what. who sees it, who stands in the window or on the porch seeing it pleased.

—

who sees it was myself on the porch first thing in the morning looking down on the garden, or from the pantry window looking out. but that was also my mother who could view the backyard when we were children, could stand at the bathroom window and have a view of the play. the play of children.

the flowers. I thought, the flowers, walking in the botanical garden with D. last Sunday. thinking of that mysterious explosion of color, but I had read that somewhere, couldn't can't remember who wrote of the explosion of color, why suddenly there were flowers in the world. and why? who would see it? if color is attractive whose eye would have been attracted? but I had been thinking of color, that poem which began as a naming of colors our student at Juvenile Hall had written the day before. she had begun with the colors but it turned into things, like 'table brown' and 'tree blue.' Fenollosa's essay, how color is not abstracted from the thing so colored, a 'non-separation.' it was E. who had been thinking of 'in my father's house there are many mansions,' she who had said to me that she had been reading the Bible. it surprised me. she was 'struck' by it, and I had also been at some time, but I was struck by her mention of it, given her politics and ideology, her skepticism. I would not have thought she had been reading the Bible. and there is the word 'struck,' in some sense a wounding. a slap in the face, a lightning bolt, some break, violence to the mind's comfortable boundaries whatever they may be. beginning with the garden, and that was my father's, complete with the snake in the backyard. lingua the tongue, but in Spanish preserves the association with language, and the whole chain begun with the thought 'fiery tongues.' hidden in that: 'naked and fiery forms.'

—

in a blind way the legend is moving.
in another task, in a moment.
in a world's war, war war t a kind of
cor an i male forgetting
another side of the face jagged cut in rock
facet that stone
o forever about grist for his mill
grind that grind that hope
fully wish (flower locked dazed)
something like a leering tongue he answered
and he arose and went unto them they at that time dwelling in
name of country
a word with you
in private
softly he shut the office door the carpet underfoot
a more delicious form of masturbation
the fish were sworded and skying and not further than a lark

wasn't
was an eyeful

haunted certain core words
decentered

at the shifting boundary
where in a starburst in a silver dollar in a candybar
where stalagmites a word associated with caves winter
the redcross the weather blue
his hand on my crotch these were loaded words I told you so
birda flying out of the mill in the desert spots on the picture
picture birds a particular
he looked down. he walked out. he cut the fish bait.
beet beet
then made over a package wrapped
signifier to signifier the signified buried
in the backyard a bottle of white rum he dug it up
and on top of that this
happened

—

San Francisco
May 20 – August 5, 1979

Beverly Dahlen was born in Portland, Oregon in November, 1934, and raised and educated in various port towns of California and the Pacific Northwest. Her previous book publications include *Out of the Third* (Momo's Press, 1974), *A Letter at Easter* (Effie's Press, 1976), and *The Egyptian Poems* (Hipparchia Press, 1983). She is an associate editor of *HOW(ever)*, a critical journal devoted to modernist and current experimental writing by women. Ms. Dahlen resides in San Francisco.

A Reading (1-7) has been produced in a first edition limited to 1250 copies of which 26 have been lettered and signed by the author and handbound by K. U. Roetzscher in green Iris cloth hardcovers with the cover design by Mary Ann Hayden mounted on a recessed panel.